your LDS

wedding
planner

a guide to a
stunning wedding day

ann louise peterson

your LDS
wedding
planner
a guide to a stunning wedding day

ann louise peterson

cfi
an imprint of cedar fort, inc.
springville, ut

ISBN 13: 978-1-4621-1016-2

Published by CFI, an imprint of Cedar Fort, Inc.
2373 W. 700 S., Springville, UT 84663
Distributed by Cedar Fort, Inc., www.cedarfort.com

LIBRARY OF CONGRESS CATALOGING-IN-PUBLICATION DATA

Peterson, Ann Louise, 1980- , author.
  Your LDS wedding planner : a guide to a stunning wedding / Ann Louise Peterson.
  pages cm
  Summary: Step by step wedding guide, from "I'm engaged" to newlywed, for the bride, groom, and other wedding party members.
  ISBN 978-1-4621-1016-2
  1. Weddings--Planning. 2. Wedding etiquette. 3. Marriage--Religious aspects--Church of Jesus Christ of Latter-day Saints. I. Title.

  HQ745.P45 2012
  395.2'2088289332--dc22

                              2011046321

Cover design by Danie Romrell
Cover design © 2012 by Lyle Mortimer
Edited and typeset by Emily S. Chambers

Printed in the United States of America

10 9 8 7 6 5 4 3 2 1

dedication

To Mom, who drilled wedding etiquette
into me since I was a fetus, and to
Patsy, who has the heart to be
her daughter-in-law's best friend.

contents

contents

introduction

Who am I? I am Ann Peterson. I love weddings, and I love lists. I've been taught my whole life about wedding etiquette. I love to help plan weddings, go to weddings, and read wedding books. But I could never find an all-inclusive book that taught the right wedding etiquette and also helped a Latter-day Saint know how to incorporate that etiquette into LDS culture. I wrote this book so people could see that wedding etiquette isn't stuffy and outdated, but will help everything run more smoothly, be even more beautiful, and—most importantly—keep this special day joyful.

Receptions are personal and all so different. They vary by region, family, culture, ethnicity, and economic status. Some wedding celebrations are full sit-down dinners, some are dances, some are open houses, and on and on. I can't hit every possible scenario. So this book is about an average, middle class, LDS wedding. Why? Because that's in the middle, it's what I know the most about, and it's my book.

You can add and subtract from my list for your wedding celebration. I'll touch on some of the optional items, but I won't focus my efforts there. The reason is that I'm trying to give a clear picture of what is culturally and socially expected and done at an LDS wedding today. Other additions are great if desired, but I'll concentrate on the things that are common enough to be expected.

Always look into your local information. Ask your friends, your family, your bishop, your ward. But think through what you want for yourself. You don't have to plan it their way—or my way, for that matter. Take it for what it's worth. Everyone is just trying to help. Remember, they all love you.

Conventions

There are a few concepts that come up over and over again, so I try to present them in a consistent way:

❑ **The Big Checklist.** These are the top level tasks of your wedding planning.

❗ **Soapbox Warning!** Of course, this whole book is my opinion. However, paragraphs that look like this contain more emotion and less reason than usual.

🕴 **For the Groom.** Most of this book is tailored to the bride, or to the bride and the groom. These paragraphs call out things that are particularly important for the groom to consider or plan for.

✍ **Note!** These are things to pay particular attention to. Snags often happen if these things are ignored.

About This Book

If you want to skip ahead and use this more as a reference than a read-it-all-the-way-through book, here's what you need to know. In the back of the book is a comprehensive checklist. Please read this checklist all the way through. The checklist is not a time line; it is meant to be used throughout the entire planning process. Each chapter of this book will outline the basics and then tune into my brain for my opinions of how to best work through each item. Remember, everything on my list is optional. Weddings are very personal and need only what you deem necessary.

This book is not so much an options book as a direction book. I don't detail for you the many different cuts and costs of wedding dresses but instead talk about the temple guidelines that should be applied to any dress.

The most important thing about your wedding day is the actual ceremony, not the decorations, the dress, the ring, or anything else. Don't let anything overshadow that wonderful and sacred event. You're getting married! Take a moment to think about how exciting that is. At the end of all this you'll be married . . . for eternity. Pretty cool.

A Few Last-Minute Technical Things

It is a good idea to get a binder to keep all your wedding planning paperwork together. This is a place to keep your budget and receipts, time line, checklists, bids, phone numbers, pictures from magazines that you want to re-create, master vendor list, everything. If you have a lot of this on the computer, keep it all together in a folder for easy retrieval. Don't forget to date revised files on the computer so you know which one you're planning from.

Consider the pros and cons to every option, especially the one you choose. You don't want any surprises later because you didn't examine all the angles.

Very few weddings (even those with professional help) go exactly as planned. Unexpected things can happen. Things could even go wrong (gasp). There might be something I'm missing (gasp, gasp). You need to decide to be happy. This day is a joyful one, and the details don't matter as much as the fact that you get to marry that wonderful man and he gets to marry you. If the cake falls or your one of your bridesmaids's dress rips or it rains, you'll still be married. Have fun. Let it be a good day. The most important thing you can control is your attitude.

chapter one

getting to know you

So, let's talk about you! Chances are, you fall into one of the following categories:

- Bride
- Groom
- Mother of the bride or groom

Let's assume you're the bride. You may not be the bride—that's okay—but don't skip this part, because it affects you too.

Congratulations! You're getting married! Marriage is the single most important relationship we embark upon. But there's a long way to go before the wedding. So, let's try to get you and your honey there in one piece.

❀ Pop Quiz!

Which of the following best describes you (the bride). Now be honest. No one's gonna tell:

A. I've dreamed about this moment all my life and I've got strong opinions and detailed plans.

B. I know I'm gonna care about the details, but I don't have a lot of plans yet.

C. I just want to get married. I might even have eloped if that word didn't sound so awful.

1

Know which one you are? Okay! Now, let's talk about how this book is going to help you.

Bride A:

You're a detail person like me. You probably got this book out of thoroughness, but you've already sketched most things out. Don't worry; we'll iron out the details together.

Please don't get overwrought if my opinions are the opposite of yours. You're the boss of your own wedding, not me.

Bride B:

This book is great for you. You're going to drive decisions, but you need help making them. I'm your virtual maid of honor, helping you make sure everything is thought of and tended to.

Bride C:

All the details in this book are optional. You can cut any of the frilly party things you don't want to do. If you're looking for a lean, meaningful wedding and reception, then I can help you get there quickly, in an orderly fashion, and with less stress and more joy.

Psst! Groom, mother of the bride! I haven't forgotten you. Much of your happiness between now and the end of the honeymoon will depend on you correctly determining which kind of bride you are attached to. Budget your disagreements with Bride A. She needs a lot of "yes, dear." Bride B needs to be kept in the loop. Give her options, and let her decide. Bride C needs few options, lots of strong recommendations, and reassurance that she will indeed survive this process. She'll probably appreciate it if you just get it done with the minimum amount of decision-making on her part.

Groom: No matter what kind of bride you are marrying, remember to give her love and cut her some slack. Planning a wedding is a stressful thing. She won't do it more than once. This is not portentous of things to come. You're both getting married, but culturally she's expected to care and be in charge while most people don't think its odd for a groom to be easygoing. Whisk her away when she needs it, and buckle down and help when that's what's called for.

Tip: This is a stressful time. A fun one, but stressful. Remember throughout your planning why you are doing this. Don't sweat the small stuff—think "big picture." And if you need a little help—

- relax and step back from it all. Take a nap or get a foot massage.
- go on a date.
- pray—the peace will come.
- read about the temple.
- read the scriptures.
- delegate and then let it go.
- expect things to go wrong, then go with it, and last
- laugh—it really is the best medicine.

Let this be a happy, enjoyable, and wonderful time. You're getting married. Yay!

chapter two

communication

When beginning the planning phase, you need to know that the key to everything is communication! Face-to-face communication (not text, email, voice mail, or even sky writing—face-to-face, eye-to-eye). Feelings get hurt fastest and easiest if you play the old whisper game. You'll never get the message across as intended if you tell someone, who needs to tell someone, who tells someone, who tells the person who needs to know. (Did you have to read that sentence more than once? It just makes my head spin.) You need to communicate openly and directly from the person who means it to the person who needs to hear it.

Communication begins with yourself. Decisions during wedding planning are relentless. How will you make all those decisions? Here are three examples of how each bride may react to communication.

✎ **Note!** This is not a surefire warning of things to come. It's a few possible pitfalls that may be avoided. Please don't be hurt; I'm not describing you. Sadly, in most cases, I'm describing myself. I'm hoping you can learn from my mistakes.

Bride A—You know what you want, and that's a great strength. Sometimes knowing what you want can be read badly by others who could perceive you as bossy or, worse, think you don't care about other people's feelings. It's all about how you say it. Just because I know what I want doesn't mean that I bowl everyone over with no care for their feelings and ideas. You may not agree with other people's opinions, but it is kind to hear them out, especially if they are contributing to the wedding, whether financially or in slave labor. They know that you know what you want. They just want to be a part of the excitement. Try to make room for their input. More people involved means more people trying to make this day special for you.

Bride B—If you care what decisions are made but aren't sure where to start or what the options are, a unique web could ensnare you. It's the "oh-don't-trouble-yourself" web. Remember, some people like to trouble themselves when it comes to weddings. For instance, if your mom lives in a different state and offers to give you a second reception that is local to her area (which is the area/ward/school that you grew up in), don't just wave her aside. She may have been asked by several people about it, or she is also very excited about your wedding and may want to participate in any way she can. Don't cut her off at the pass because you fear she might be inconveniencing herself. If she offers, then she's not inconvenienced. She wants to help make your day as special as possible.

Bride C—Sometimes being unsure of or even not caring about every decision, you can lean toward just trying to make everyone else happy. You want to please all those input givers. Be careful. There's a reason there's only one CEO. Someone has to be the boss and make the actual decision. It's wonderful to get advice from people, but know that you can never possibly make every single person happy, and it's really most important that you be happy on your wedding day. If trying to please everyone is stressing you out and making you sad, then choose what makes you the happiest, even if it upsets someone else. With some people, you can never win. It's best to enjoy this most spectacular day of your life.

To All Brides—Don't try to do too much. When you think about "folding each napkin into a flower," does it excite you or does it make your head explode? If you don't care about something, then let it go. Either don't have it at all or let someone else take care of it. If

5

you just can't make one more decision, then don't. Determine what matters the most to you at the beginning and start there. That way you don't burn out before you get to the things that matter the most.

You may have known your whole life exactly what your wedding was going to be like, or you may simply have a few clippings of cakes or bouquets you admire, or you may have never thought it over. Take some time to mull over some general thoughts before you have to decide. What kind of reception, dress, colors, flowers do you want? Look through options. That way, when it's "final answer" time, you can make an informed decision. Then once you've chosen, let it be done. You can change you mind, of course, but try to decide fully before ordering, reserving, or buying. Don't stress yourself out by second-guessing yourself. What you've chosen is beautiful, I promise. Let yourself relax and be at peace. It's going to be a magnificent day.

Communication is most important between the engaged couple. You—the bride and groom—have a few things that you should discuss. Likely you already know things like each other's last name and who your favorite childhood pet was, but let's talk about the things that most impact a marriage. If you've already talked about these things, awesome! You're ahead of the game. If not, find some quiet time to talk to each other about these things.

- **The Gospel**—Share your testimony with each other. Talk about how important regular Sunday attendance and temple attendance are to you. How do you go about fulfilling your callings? Will you sustain one another?
- **Money**—Who will provide for the family and for how long? How will you handle money? Who will pay the bills? Will you have a budget that you adhere to? How will you handle money problems? Decide here and now to always pay your tithing. This will be the easiest time to make that decision.
- **Your Career Goals**—What are your ambitions and how close are you to them?
- **School**—Do you still need to finish college? How long do you have left? How important is education to you?
- **Work**—How will you divide the family work? Who cooks? Who cleans? Who takes care of the yard?
- **Family**—This has two parts: the families you are coming from

and the family you are beginning. First, the family you are coming from: How important will their input be? How will you handle the holidays? How often will you visit them? Second, your new family: How soon do you want to start having children? Do you want a big family or a small one? Who will stay home with the children? How will you handle discipline?

- **Arguing**—How do you fight? Do you storm off or plant your feet and tough it out? Do you need time to cool off?
- **Intimacy**—How often do you anticipate being intimate? Are there aspects you are uncomfortable with? How will you handle birth control? hahaha
- **Outside Interests**—Do you have similar interests? If not, how will you feed your interests without hurting your marriage? For example, will I still have scrapbook night every Friday with the girls and will you still have Monday night football with the guys? Communication, intimacy, and money are the top things that impact the happiness of a marriage. It will benefit you in the long run to talk about these things before they are even a problem.

❑ Decide for yourselves (the couple) what type of wedding you are hoping for.

You two as a couple are about to answer a plethora of questions. It's a good idea to have a couple of general ideas in mind to guide you along your way. Realize that the final decisions will be made later, but you need a rough idea. So:

- Do you want a big or small wedding?
- What are you trying to do for your guests? Feed them? Entertain them? Give them a place to bring you congratulations and many presents? Whatever the answer, you need to know it.
- What's most important to you? I hope the answer to this is, "Oh, Ann, being married is most important to me and all this other stuff is just frills." That's right. Good. It's okay, I love the frills too. Just ask my husband. I'm all for a big hoopla, but let's not lose sight of the point, right? Basically

you want to at least briefly discuss with each other what you are hoping for. Be careful to keep your expectations in the same ballpark as your projected budget. Ask the groom how involved he wants to be. Does he care? Or would he rather have all of his toenails and fingernails slowly and systematically removed? It's okay, but it's good to know, right?

A word to the groom: Your beautiful bride has been looking forward to this day for her entire life. She planned this day with every pack of girlfriends who ever accompanied her to the ladies room while at a party. It matters to her, so even if the details don't matter to you, try to help her. If you don't want to be involved in the planning and she doesn't mind, great. Lucky you. But if you don't want to be involved and she wants desperately for you to care if she chooses roses or lilacs, try to care. Oh, and try to pick the one you know she likes better. Hint: It's the one that makes her eyes glow.

❏ Parents of the bride and groom meet together with the bride and groom to determine the overall budget and how the expenses will be shared

Groom's side traditionally pays for tuxedos, bride's bouquet, bride's ring, luncheon, honeymoon, and marriage license.

I'm placing this checkbox in the communication chapter, because communication can make this a wonderful or very tense meeting. This meeting is just the bride, groom, and their parents. That's it. No wedding planners or other outside influences yet. This meeting is first and foremost to help make your wedding less stressful and more joyful for all parties involved. It is important at this exciting time to take a couple of hours (And it will be hours—bring snacks for the men. Lots of snacks.) and have all parties meet together. Bring your wedding binder, calendars, magazine clippings, and a notebook. Alert everyone as to what you expect to accomplish at this meeting so they'll come prepared. Have them bring their calendars and notebooks too. It will be a night of decisions. This meeting can accomplish a few different things.

First, it can give everyone a chance to meet, should they not have met before. Let them see each other face-to-face and share in the engaged couple's excitement.

Second, you can begin to discuss a possible date, time, and place for the wedding. Also begin to make some of those decisions that barricade the way to further truth and light, like who's in the wedding party.

Third, it gives everyone a chance to put their oar in. Everyone involved will have thoughts about how they think this whole wedding is going to go down. No matter who's paying for it, everyone has an opinion. This is a time to hear what they all think and to hear any offers of "My friend's hairdresser's visiting teacher makes wedding cakes!"

Fourth, and most important, it is a time to determine the budget and make decisions about how the expenses will be shared. This must be determined directly among the paying parties. (See Budget chapter for more insights.) This will help to avoid hurt feelings, anger, and annoyance at perceived "meddling" in someone else's responsibilities. Having said that, once the decision is made of who is responsible for what, don't continue to tell the other planners how to plan their portion of the wedding. (So Mom, let the mom-in-law handle her stuff, and you handle yours. Don't worry; the bride's on top of it.)

Now, the time may come, as it often does, that the parents of the bride need to speak to the parents of the groom. (Such as, "Hey, wanna go shopping for our mother's dresses together?") Many people believe that the parents need to talk to each other only through the engaged couple. This is wrong. The parents should be able to talk directly to each other. The best way to work through a problem is to speak to the source. However, should there be a problem, the bride and groom may have a certain level of understanding about their parents and could help in the communication. Remember, Mom, your bride-daughter will have some insights into her future in-laws' lives and ways of dealing with things. Her advice could be invaluable. When a situation arises where there is need for communication, perhaps let all parties involved be present, instead of a lot of he-said, she-said.

! So, for My First General Soapbox Warning

Remember, bride, that you are not the only one getting married. This is your groom's day too. You love him a lot, right? You think he's cute? Think of his dimples. His opinions aren't meaningless. Let him in on the decisions. If he's not interested, then you can run with it. But if he is, including him will start off your marriage better. Involve him in the preparations. We want it to be a joyful day for all involved, not a day for the bride only while the groom gets run over and pushed around. That's not the way a marriage should be, so why have it start that way with your wedding?

Enough of that.

Remember also that everyone involved in the planning of this event will be your family when this is over. Try hard to keep some peace. Be sensitive to issues involving divorce, remarriages, and death. And be extra sensitive to your future mother-in-law. She will be your family for eternity and will always be your sweetie's mom. She's loved him a long time. She's cleaned up his throw up and prayed for him night and day, so don't forget her feelings as well.

Having said this, you can't please everyone. Don't rethink decisions so much that you waste time and money and upset all parties involved. Be decisive but get the information first. And remember that the opinion of the person holding the purse strings matters a bit more than everyone else's opinion, except the bride.

As I mentioned before, don't try to do it all yourself, bride or mom. However, decide carefully who you ask to help. Choose people you strongly believe will follow through. Be very specific in what you ask of them. Communicate clearly. People have different ideas about what the same thing means.

Tip: Once you decide who's in charge of what, write their name next to the checkbox on my list. That way you'll remember who has what assignment when it gets to "go time."

❑ Decide who's in charge

This may seem like a no-brainer after the previous checkbox, but let's elaborate. You need to know: Who's decision is the final decision? Who's responsibility is it to get the task done? Who will troubleshoot any problems? The answer to these questions is not exclusively the person who is paying. The bride and groom's wishes must always be taken into account, yet they needn't be responsible for all troubleshooting.

Are you going to use a wedding coordinator or organize the vendors and all the arrangements yourself? Are you even going to use vendors? These questions can be answered differently for each section of the wedding, such as, "yes, we're using a caterer, but my aunt is doing the flowers."

One word of advice. You need someone in charge on the wedding day. Someone who can fix problems and who has access to emergency funds or options. This person should not be the bride, groom, or their parents. Those people will be too busy on the wedding day with greeting their guests, not to mention the actualities of getting married and the reception. Determine someone else to be in charge and let everyone else know who that person is so order can be maintained. But make the duties clear to that person so the power doesn't go to his head and they start changing things you have already set in place.

In your search for the right person, especially if you are going with a professional wedding coordinator, look for

- **Availability**—can they even give you the time?
- **Cost**—if using a professional, get a detailed estimate in writing that is clear on what she will provide, how much it costs, and when payment is due.
- **Acceptance** of your plans and budget (especially your emergency budget and how it may be spent, as they may be in charge of that).
- **Easy to contact**—you need to be able to stay in contact with this person.
- **Personality**—make sure you like this person and can work with him or her.

❑ Double and maybe even triple check all reservations and arrangements.

This includes the florist, photographer, temple, reception

location, caterer, cake, decorations, band, honeymoon, and any others.

This must be done whether you are using professionals or not. It is actually done both throughout the process and very near the wedding, but it's important to make sure everyone is on the same page and planning on the same thing you're planning on. You'd hate to be counting on someone or something and have it fall through because someone wrote down the wrong date, time, color, or flavor.

chapter three

budget

How Much Should It Cost?

There is no regular amount that a wedding is supposed to cost. It could be free (well, the cost of a marriage license) or cost millions. Doing a small amount of research, before determining your budget, to estimate a few of the major costs will help this go smoother and faster. Set a budget that can get you close to what you want but that is realistic and practical. A wedding can be wonderful at many different levels. You just need to see who all is pitching in financially and if your dream wedding has to be planned for next to nothing or at Prince William's forty-plus-million-dollar budget. (By the way, if you have his budget, will you adopt me?)

Very important! When asking family members or friends to help with either plans or actual aspects of the wedding (for example: photography, cake, flowers, catering), you need to be prepared for problems. This isn't to say that something will go wrong; it means that you need to decide that it's okay with you if it does go wrong. If subpar results are simply unacceptable, then pay for a professional. It is commonly believed that going with a friend, family member, or ward member is best because it's free. There is always a cost, but it may not be financial. You need to decide that if something totally stinks, you'll still love the person and not be mad. This is the cost of having a friend or family member help you instead of hiring a professional. Also, be clear as to if and when this person will get paid and exactly how much. These are areas of an uncomfortable nature to discuss with family members and close friends after the fact.

Where Do I Start?

Prioritize, prioritize, prioritize. Decide how important things are to you and budget more for those things. For example, do you want more people there or a finer menu? A long, exotic honeymoon or an expensive wedding ring? Think about what you'll look back on and care about. Ask your parents what they wish they had done. Remember that money is an exhaustible resource, so choose wisely what matters most.

❏ Make a prioritized rough budget

Divide the potential costs into
- What I need
- What I want

(from most important to me down to least important to me)

Don't forget to add in little things like cake-cutting utensils, your garter, and gratuity for any venders. Then determine what your resources are (including money, talents, connections, and current assets). Once you've prioritized, budget the most money for the things that matter the most to you. Then work your way down the priority list until either the funds or the expenses run out. If your budget is small, there are many ways to stretch your dollar. Use a free venue or have a friend with an awesome playlist serve as DJ. Some things can be scrimped on, and other things can be dropped altogether. Simply decide what's important to you and make it work by cutting back on other items.

Who's Going to Pay for All This?

The wedding expenses are being shared differently nowadays. The traditional division of expenses is groom (or groom's side of the family)—bride's ring, tuxedos, wedding luncheon or rehearsal dinner, marriage license, the bride's bouquet (some people extend this to all flowers), and the honeymoon. Bride—everything else. But this is just a starting point. Grooms are paying for more and more, and often families don't get involved in the finances at all, leaving it all up to the engaged couple. Whichever way you split it, no other decisions should be made until a budget has been set.

Note! If your parents are paying for your reception and you are having more than one reception, it is only within their etiquette responsibility to cover the reception they are hosting.

Bringing the budget up at the parent meeting will give your parents a chance to offer to pay for things or for you to ask them if they are interested in contributing. Be careful though. If your parents don't have a lot to donate financially, this could be a touchy subject. Help to ease the blow by not announcing your dream wedding and looking at them expectantly. Try to ease into your desires, maybe giving them a chance to offer anything they are able to do. If they don't have a lot to donate financially but still want to help, be gracious and try to find a way for them to donate physically to the wedding. For instance, they could help set up the reception tables or address invitations.

The parent meeting is the time to decide (not only discuss—decide) if the expenses will or will not be split the traditional way. It has become common for the groom's side to pay for more as their wedding cost responsibilities are traditionally smaller. However, do not offer to pitch in to pay more because you don't think the other party is paying enough or making a big enough gesture of grandeur. For instance, if you think the luncheon should be at a five-star restaurant and the paying party chooses a homemade meal in a church, do not offer to pay so that it can be "better." That can be rude and offensive. Money may not have been the deciding factor. Always give your input, and tell them what you are hoping for, but remember people celebrate differently. I love a party with a million people around me, while my husband would rather a small intimate gathering with great food and music. Let the parents's tastes and comfort be a factor as well. Also, if you know someone's budget is straining, try to be considerate and choose the most cost-effective yet still beautiful option. However, the opposite is also true. If Mom offers to pay a caterer and decorator so she can enjoy the day and not worry about the details, let her. You may not be helping her by having the family do more work in setup and cooking. This can add stress and extra steps. If she's willing to pay for it to make it more convenient, I figure the easy answer is, "Thanks, Mom!"

If you are paying for your own wedding without financial help, which is becoming quite common, then it's best to talk it over as a couple. Finances are a common problem that people don't approach in the same way. Do you want to spend more on the wedding and he wants to spend less, saving more for your marriage? You'll need to come to a compromise that you both feel good about. Don't over-spend and send yourself into debt. When all is said and done, you want a marriage, not a giant credit card bill. Also, it would be kind to ask your parents for advice and opinions to keep them involved. They might have helpful ideas for you. They will be flattered to have you ask for their advice and wisdom.

The people that love you (such as your parents) may want to throw you a party at their expense. That's really sweet. Consider let-ting them. This could include the reception, the luncheon, or the showers. You, as the bride, don't need to be responsible for all of the party planning. If you're overwhelmed, delegate. It's really key to helping you find joy in the whole process instead of stress. You don't have to set up all the decorations yourself. However, remember that if your parents are paying for your wedding, they get a say in how the money is spent. Still want to keep control? Assign a trusted family member to investigate caterers and bring you the top three choices. This saves you time, involves others, and lets you make the decision. If Mom wants more control and she's paying, then try reversing the previous scenario. You pick your top three favorites (with emphasis on your top choice) and have her choose. That way you still get one of your favorites, and she gets to decide how her money is spent.

❑ Set a clear & specific budget

No matter who ends up paying for the wedding, an amount needs to be chosen that all paying parties are comfortable with and that doesn't put anyone into debt.

Okay, now here's the key—the most important thing. Are you listening?

🖎 **Stay within your set budget.** It's hard to know beforehand exactly how much everything will cost. If you end up going over budget in one area, you'll have to trim somewhere else. As you create your budget, give yourself a miscellaneous section to provide you with some wiggle room, also leaving you a little extra for any hidden or unexpected expenses (such as taxes or gratuities). This will help you stay balanced. Remember, you decided at the beginning what you could afford. It's best to stick with it.

With food, centerpieces, decorations, flowers, and even the cake, presentation is everything. You can use inexpensive things arranged in a beautiful way and no one will be the wiser.

How Do I Keep Track of My Spending?

Keep a collective budget tracking sheet. (Refer to the back of this book for a sample budget.) Keep track of everything you are spending and when others are spending your money as well. (You don't want to have your sister arrange for the band and find out at the last minute that it cost twice the price you were budgeting.)

Save receipts, contracts, and bids. Mark down on the budget tracking sheet when a deposit has been paid, how much it is, how much is still owed, and when payment is due in full.

Other Budget Advice

Assume that things will cost more than you think they will, especially all the little things. They sure add up. I'd rather be pleasantly surprised when something costs less than the budgeted amount than the other way around.

Ask yourself from time to time along the way, "Is this worth the cost or effort?" It will help you keep things in perspective.

A budget is not a requirement to spend. If you don't need all the funds allocated to a particular aspect, then stash them away. You can use them for extra honeymoon souvenirs, household items, rent, tuition, or even start saving for a home.

The words "wedding" or "bridal" add dollar signs to your bids. Don't be afraid to look at other kinds of caterers, photographers, bakeries, and so on.

Vendors

Shop around. Three is a good number of vendors to seriously consider. Look at as many as you like superficially, but three is a great sample size for getting specifics and bids. Be open with the vendors about seeking other help. Competition may encourage them to drop the price or throw in a few extras. Always ask vendors what is included in the price. Ask them if that price is the best they can do. They may drop it. It's also not a bad idea to ask for other advantages or inclusions to the same price.

Note! Get all bids, along with their inclusions, in writing and never sign anything without reading it carefully.

It might be written in a contract that the vendor can substitute other goods or services. Get specific and ask many questions. A warning: if a deal looks too good to be true, it just might be.

Know when and if deposits will be required and when the full balance will be due. If the balance will be due at the wedding, have the checks prewritten and organized into envelopes with the vendors' names on the front. Include any gratuities as well. Make it someone else's job to distribute these envelopes at the event, but be sure it's someone reliable. This is traditionally the best man's responsibility but can be done by anyone you trust such as a parent or other family member.

chapter four
before invitations

☑ Set a date *August 8ᵗʰ*

No matter how long you have before the big day, there are a certain number things that have to be done. It's just a matter of how fast you have to do them. How long should your engagement be? I think, the shorter the better, but long enough. You do need enough time to get everything accomplished, but if your engagement is very long, you'll find yourself with time to spare. It doesn't take an entire year. Really. My advice for the shortest engagement is probably two months. (Even this is short. You'll be focused almost solely on wedding prep, but it can be done.) A better estimate for not going crazy is more like four to six months. The simple answer is, if you don't have a lot of time, then you usually do less or you share the load and delegate a lot more.

No matter how much time you have, start early. It will reduce your stress. As the days disappear, more things than you expect will spring onto your to-do list. The things that take the longest are: compiling guest lists, addressing invitations, and above all, making a decision and sticking to it. A special consideration to setting the date is that keeping the law of chastity gets harder and harder the longer you have to wait. Make sure it's a reasonable amount of time to get things done and to stay chaste.

The date of your wedding may affect the cost. If your wedding is near Mother's Day, the flowers will be marked up. If your wedding is

May (ish) 10ᵗʰ

near Valentine's Day, almost everything will be marked up. Believe me. My anniversary is February 15th.

Your reception doesn't need to be the same day as your wedding. You can have it the next day, the next week, even the next month. Remember that if it's immediately following your honeymoon, you'll have less involvement with last-minute details, as you'll be out of touch.

If you are going to be traveling a fair distance to the temple, you need to make sure you have enough time on your wedding day. In this case it might be easier overall to split up the ceremony and reception between two days. But you'll want to make sure the right dates get out to the right guests.

Once you have set the date, some people like to send save-the-date cards. These are primarily used to alert important members of the wedding party that will have to make travel plans. Save-the-date cards aren't required or expected. If sent, they don't go out to everyone, just those who need warning of date and location details, although everyone who gets a save-the-date card must receive an invitation to the wedding.

Do you need to announce your wedding? That is totally up to you and to what is culturally expected in your area. You could call everyone you know, put an announcement in the local paper, or have an engagement party and shout it from the rooftops. Engagement parties are becoming less and less common, but any way you'd like to celebrate your engagement is just great, although not required or expected.

❑ Determine the wedding party

Who is in the wedding party? The wedding party consists of all the people closely associated to the wedding: the bride, groom, mothers, fathers, any attendants, siblings, and best friends. The people that will be included in all aspects of the wedding day constitute the wedding party. Or, simply stated, all immediate players in the wedding.

Usually in a civil wedding, the bride and groom have bridesmaids and groomsmen, and all of them wear matching dresses and tuxes. These attendants are followed down the aisle by a cute tux-wearing

ring bearer and an adorable tiny flower girl. In an LDS temple wedding, we don't have an aisle with flowers thrown or need ring bearers or attendants; thus it can be difficult to mesh this tradition with our culture. Many people still have all these attendants stand in their wedding line, creating a need for the matching dresses and tuxes.

It is important to decide who will be a part of the wedding party early in the planning stages. As word of your engagement spreads, people will start to wonder if they are going to be a part of it and, if so, how big a part.

My opinion is that attendants are optional and not necessary in an LDS temple wedding. They often add problems and questions and increase the number of people that you have to try to keep happy. But if you are going to have attendants, such as a maid of honor, bridesmaids, and groomsmen, then use them for at least some of their intended purposes. Don't just create a need to make more decisions on matching dresses and tuxes and not get anything out of it. Put them to work.

You'll need to decide which attendants you want to have, who you want to fill those positions, what you want their roles to be (Will they be worker bees? Will they stand in the receiving line?), and how you want them to look. (Do they have to match or each have their own bouquet?)

You can use your attendants as much or as little as you like. Your mom, best friends, sisters, future in-laws, and fellow Relief Society sisters will all be willing to pitch in without an official job title. Should you decide to have attendants, don't forget to think about your family. If you don't want to use your family as attendants, find another way to help them feel needed and included, especially your parents. Here are some of my suggestions for tasks for the attendants:

Maid (or Matron) of Honor

- help address invitations
- organize a bridal shower
- obtain her own wedding attire
- organize the bridesmaids' attire
- supervise bridesmaids in their duties

- handle any issues raised by the bridesmaids
- keep track of groom's wedding ring on the wedding day
- manage the bride's personal items at the reception
- help keep the bride on schedule
- attend all wedding celebrations
- assist in any prewedding errands or decisions
- if desired, handle the cleaning/return of the wedding dress
- assist in postwedding cleanup

Bridesmaids

- help address invitations
- assist in the bridal shower
- assist the bride and maid of honor in any prewedding tasks and errands
- attend all wedding day celebrations
- obtain their own wedding attire
- assist in postwedding cleanup

Best Man

- obtain personal wedding attire
- organize groomsmen's attire
- supervise groomsmen's duties
- handle any issues raised by the groomsmen
- manage groom's personal items at the reception
- keep the groom on schedule
- attend all wedding celebrations
- assist in any prewedding errands or decisions
- return the groom's tux
- make sure groom has marriage license on wedding day
- keep track of bride's wedding ring on the wedding day
- offer first toast (if doing toasts)

- help groom plan honeymoon details
- make sure corsages and boutonnieres get passed out to the right people
- help gather the wedding party for photos
- manage checks for vendors on the wedding day
- assist in postwedding cleanup

Groomsmen

- assist the groom and best man in any prewedding tasks and errands
- attend all wedding day celebrations
- obtain their own wedding attire
- usher VIP guests (including elderly and disabled) throughout the wedding day
- help direct any guests to the next site of the day
- transport gifts at the end of the night
- assist in postwedding cleanup

Remember, these are suggestions, and a small list at that. You can have anyone help in any way that is actually helpful, but let people help you. Give the attendants each other's contact information so they can work through some things without you, such as the bridal shower. Be careful who you enlist. They should take pressures away from you, not add to them. Select the wedding party as soon as possible and ask them if it's okay. They need to understand the time and financial requirements that will accompany their position.

❑ Make a tentative "months to the wedding" schedule

It is a good idea to make a tentative schedule for the months leading up to the wedding—a countdown or time line, however you wish to look at it. Take out a calendar and decide when you'll have the engagement shoot completed, the guest lists compiled, the invitations mailed, and so forth. This will help you stay on track through the planning process.

You do not need to choose a due date for each and every check box. Refer to my suggested time frame in Appendix B for more specific help on this. No matter how much time you have before the wedding, you'll need to budget your time and energy as much as your money. Prioritize your time as you did your money. Get the most important things done first and work your way down to the extras.

In appendix B, I have given some suggestions as to how soon you should be doing each of your checkbox steps. These are merely suggestions. Use the things that apply to your wedding. You really need to decide how much time you're going to give to each step to help you not get behind and thus overwhelmed, and then you can delegate the rest of the tasks. Once you've delegated to someone, let them take care of it. Micromanaging doesn't remove the stress from your plate.

❑ Make a tentative "day of" schedule

This is just to get the ball rolling. Refer to the back of this book for a sample "day of" schedule. Making a "day of" schedule will not only make everything run more smoothly, it will also assure you that you've thought of everything, and help you determine what really matters to you. As you mentally run through the entire actual event, you will notice if anything has been overlooked.

If you get stuck on what comes next, try starting at the end of the night and working your way back, making time for the different elements of the reception. One great thing about this method is that it helps you see how early you have to start in order to fit everything in. Don't forget to build in time to rest.

☒ Choose a temple Newport Beach, CA

The best choice for a temple is usually the temple district you are in. However, the bride and groom are usually not from the same temple district. Generally the temple closest to the bride is chosen, but it's up to you. A temple is a temple is a temple.

❑ Schedule the temple

✍ **Schedule the temple!** For real. You can't get married if you don't.

You need to schedule the temple before printing the date on your invitations. Some temples have certain times for live sealings, or it may be closed for cleaning. You'll want to check. Better safe than sorry.

Before calling the temple, you have some homework to do. Your preparation will help the phone call to the temple go faster and be a much more joyful experience.

Information to gather (for both the bride and the groom):

- **Full name**
  First, middle, last—not a nickname, a full name, like on your birth certificate

- **Date of birth**
  Month, day, year

- **Membership number**
  If you are endowed, this number is on your temple recommend. If not, your number can be obtained from your bishop or ward clerk.

- **Phone numbers**
  Home and cell phone for both of you and possibly home phones for your parents.

- **Mailing address**

- **Current ward and stake**

- **Your wedding date**

- **An approximate time of day** August 8th *morning*
  Remember to be flexible on your time or you may have to be flexible on your date. The temple will do their best to meet your needs. When choosing a time, it's good to keep in mind that you'll have to be to the temple one hour early, so if you want a 7 a.m. sealing, you'll need to be up, ready to go (hair, make-up, breakfast, everything), and at the temple by 6 a.m. at the latest.

- **An approximate number of guests** make list ...
  Check with both your mom and your sweetie's mom to get a rough guess of how many temple guests to expect. Limit your guests to your very closest family members only. This will help you determine how big a room you require. Each sealing room

has a specific seating capacity. Be flexible about your number of guests.

- **Have you been a member of the Church for over a year?**
If you or your groom is a recent convert, the temple will ask for a confirmation date.

- **Is this a first temple marriage for both of you?**
If not, then there will be a whole series of other questions, regarding how the previous marriage was terminated (death or divorce) and if First Presidency approval is required.

- **Are both of you endowed?**

With this information, scheduling the temple should be a snap. But remember to get the information for both you and your groom. You'd be surprised which questions trip up brides the most, like "What's your groom's full name?"

Lastly, the temple will send you a packet of information.

✎ **Read the temple letters as soon as you get them and read them carefully!**

You would be surprised how many brides think they know what it says and head to the temple, only to end up in tears when the matron stops her at the door and tells her that she can't get married because she didn't abide by the rules. Believe me, it has happened and will continue to happen. You think you know everything it says. You don't. Bride: read the letter. Groom: read the letter. Bride's Mom: read the letter. Groom's Mom: read the letter. Read the letter. Please. Don't say I didn't warn you. And more importantly, don't say the temple didn't warn you.

❑ Take engagement photos

You'll want to get this done right away, as it will hold up the invitation process. Doing it early will also give you plenty of time to choose a picture you both like or to have retakes if you don't like any of the first batch. If you're trying to cut costs, the engagement photos are a great time to have a photography-savvy friend help instead of having them be your wedding photographer. (See photography chapter.)

The engagement photos are a lot less formal, and you have several photos to choose from. Besides, if you don't like any, you can just take them again. Engagement photos don't need to be taken in a studio. This is a time to have a little more fun and to be creative. Let these photos reflect you as a couple. But be careful not to go too over the top. For many people, this photo will be their only impression of you.

❑ Register with a store

This is not necessary.

Should you choose to register, bride and groom should go together to register. Select a store based on these questions:

- **How often do they update their registry?**
  Most guests will purchase their gifts within a day or two of your wedding. If the store only updates their list once a day, you'll have a lot of repeats. Look for a store that updates by the transaction or several times in one day.

- **How much do you like the store's overall merchandise?**
  Several people will simply buy you gift cards to the store you register at. If you don't like the store for anything more than what you registered for, it can be tricky to use up hundreds of dollars in gift cards there.

- **What's their return policy like? Do you need a gift receipt to prove your item was purchased there? How flexible are they?**
  You'll be surprised how stingy some stores can be.

❗ Soapbox Warning

Not so long ago, people used wedding registries so the couple could choose a china pattern, crystal, or silver set, and guests could purchase one small piece at a time, providing the couple with a complete matched set. This is a much less common use of a registry now. They have become a greedy wish list, made by the bride and groom happily skipping through the store scanning each and every item they could ever imagine wanting within one, two, or even three stores. It is totally inappropriate to include: DVDs, games, candy, liquor, or contraceptives on a wedding registry (all of which I've seen.) My suggestion would be, should you choose to have a wedding registry, be conservative. This is a way for guests at your wedding to know which items you need, not everything and anything you want. Remember that most of your guests (who are friends to your parents and future in-laws) will have only this registry list as an impression of you. Gifts should be an expression of the giver not chosen off the receiver's list of acceptable items. Think as you make your list. You are just giving them an idea of what you need. If you put towels on the list, they know you need towels. You don't have to pick out your three acceptable colors that match your dream color scheme and put all of them on your list. And last, please review your list before exiting the store—you may not remember or realize everything you've scanned.

Some Things to Keep in Mind

- Try to choose things at varying prices. This will make it easier for different people to choose a gift. Don't be afraid to put a few big items on the list, such as a nice pot set or vacuum. Groups will often buy these bigger items together.
- Think of the space in your new home. If you won't have room for an item, you probably shouldn't register for it.
- Last, how are you going to alert people as to where you are registered? Traditionally and etiquette-wise, you are not supposed to put an insert in the wedding invitation. That is, however, very common and generally accepted. But there are some alternatives. Use your wedding party to spread the word through "word of mouth." Give your mom and future mother-in-law registry cards to pass out to any friends who might ask. You can also include registry cards in your bridal shower invitations or, in our technological world, you can put it on a wedding website or even Facebook. Voila! Everyone knows.

❏ ♦ Arrange the wedding luncheon location
(Can put off if sending separate invitations)

The luncheon has taken the place of the traditional rehearsal dinner in many areas. In the LDS culture we encourage getting married in the temple and so do not require a rehearsal. Most LDS families do choose a time to share a meal together around the wedding. This has become a time for the bride and groom to share their first meal together. However, this can be done as a dinner the night before the wedding or a "luncheon" on the wedding day between the ceremony and the reception. You could also do a breakfast. Whatever time of day you choose, most of the same things that I say apply. I will be referring to it as a "luncheon" from here on out. If coming right from the temple and going from there to the reception, then take into account location compared to the ceremony and reception sites. Also give extra time between the ceremony and the "luncheon" for pictures and changing of clothes, but be respectful of your wedding guests waiting for their meal.

❑ 👤 Choose a time for the luncheon
(can be put off, if sending separate invitations)

Remember that if you are serving a full meal at your reception, that may impact the time and day that you want to do the wedding "luncheon." (Refer to chapter eight for more on the wedding luncheon.)

❑ Select a place for the reception Mission Inn + ...

There are so many wonderful and beautiful options. Of course, there are pros and cons to each. Many people use their church. Other choices could be: gardens, college buildings, museums, backyards, club houses, hotels, government buildings, parks. The list truly goes on.

When choosing a place for your reception, you want to think through several things. This decision is one of the first that can strongly affect the joyfulness of your wedding experience. People often choose their reception venue based on beauty or a girlish dream to "just have my wedding reception there or I'll die." Lots of factors should be taken into account before settling on and reserving a reception venue.

- **Cost:** This goes back to your budget. If you have the budget for a large reception center and it will ease the stress of the parties involved in setup and take down, then go for it. The most common and cheapest alternative is probably your basic ward house or stake center. However, some people then spend lots of money renting special decorations to spruce up the building. This could end up making it cheaper overall (and much less trouble) to just go with a reception center in the first place. Be sure to ask what is included in the cost and watch out for hidden costs. Things may or may not be included that you expected.

- **Location:** You want to choose a place that is a reasonable drive for your guests and wedding party. It should also be fairly closely related to the locations of your ceremony and wedding luncheon. You will also want to think, "How am I going to explain this location to all of my guests? Is a simple address enough or is it difficult to find?"

! Soapbox Warning

Okay, I know that there are plenty of beautiful venues out there. And you can use them if you are rolling in dough and want to simplify things for yourself. But I've seen many a bride force her family, or worse—her prospective in-laws—into shelling out beaucoup bucks for a venue that none of them could afford and that really inconvenienced everyone involved. You really can have a beautiful reception in a "plain ol'" meetinghouse. I know, I know, it looks like a cultural hall. But that's one of the things it's there for. It has tons of parking, beautiful grounds, a sound system, and a giant room in the middle that's totally suited to such a thing. Plus—it's free! It can really be improved and embellished for little cost and lots of imagination. Oh yeah, and it's conveniently located to yourself, your ward members, and many of your close friends . . . I mean, how awesome is that?

- **Availability:** You'll want to see if your chosen venue is even available for receptions at the time of year or the time of day that you are requesting. When will you be allowed into the venue for setup?
- **Space:** Is there enough room for what you envision? Room for tables and chairs? A dance floor? A buffet table? Your guests too? Make sure you can see the layout of your reception, at least superficially, in this particular space.

- **Policies:** Facilities tend to have policies about number of people, kinds of decorations allowed, and the time you are allowed to come in and start. You may not be able to have all the things you desire, such as open-flame candles. Best to get a list of rules. Make sure you have all the details lined out and signed on so you know what to expect and you don't get any surprises later.

- **Ability or necessity to decorate:** Some people choose a reception center because they don't have to decorate, whereas, going to the ward house will require decorations. An outside reception in a garden or backyard also requires less decorating, and therefore you save on flowers and decor (assuming you don't re-landscape for the event). Think also about the time needed to decorate and cleanup, not to mention extra time for pictures. It is difficult to get all these things done in just a couple of hours. You'll need your venue reserved for a least the full wedding day. Lots of people reserve the night before as well in order to go in early to decorate.

- **Catering:** Almost all reception halls require you to use their catering and/or have minimum charges, making this a necessary consideration when choosing your venue.

- **Food preparation facilities:** If you don't have to use their catering, do they have kitchen facilities for your use? Consider food preparation, service, and maintenance of temperature.

- **Clean-up:** As mentioned before, you'll need to allow time for clean-up, unless, of course, the reception hall takes care of this for you. (Many reception halls will setup and cleanup for an added fee.)

- **Weather:** This is especially a concern if you're going for an outdoor affair. Remember that weather is unpredictable, and it's important to have a backup plan. You may have more to worry about than rain—there's always the chance of wind, humidity, tornado, and even skunk smell. Okay, it's hard to prepare for that last one. You will also want to consider weather, even if you are indoors. Weather will affect your guests' commute and parking as well.

- **Parking:** If you are having your reception at a ward house or stake center, then parking is generally not a problem. However, I have been to many a reception in a beautiful backyard, where I am forced to trek half a mile in high heels, carting four children and a gift in 95-degree weather, because no neighborhood is built to allow for three hundred cars at one single house. That can take away from the joyful atmosphere you are going for. The last thing you want is angry and annoyed guests. If you are having a backyard reception, warn your neighbors, park your own cars elsewhere, and provide people to help with heavy gifts, long walks, or extremes in hot or cold weather. Also, sometimes a reception center is located in a city where parking is difficult and guests may even have to pay to park. This should be taken into account as well. If you want to use a venue with difficult parking options, you have options too. A recent reception in a backyard had limited parking, and the guests were required to park up to a full mile away. The bridal family had arranged to have boys drive golf carts back and forth down the neighborhood streets to pick up guests and bring them to and from the reception. What a great idea! That's using your noggin.

- **Decoration placement:** If using a reception hall, they will guide you through this step. If using a ward house or backyard or some such venue, you'll want to take a look around and decide if there is really room for all you envision. (Receiving line, cake table, gift table, tables for eating, dancing area, band, throne room. Okay, I threw that last one in just to see if you were paying attention.) Especially, is there room for all of your guests?

- **Flow of guests:** You'll want to pay attention to your entrances and exits. You don't want your guests to have to fight the line coming in just to get out and go home.

- **Handicap accessibility:** You'll need to make sure that there is handicap parking. Also, you'll need to make sure these guests can get in or out of the building doors and up and down levels. Think about not only wheelchairs but also older people using canes, those who have trouble walking, or guests who have poor eyesight. Cobblestones can be problematic, as can dark entrances.

- **Potties:** Let's face it, you're going to need them. Know where the available potties are and how accessible they are to your guests and yourself.

- **The public:** How public is your location? Is it a historical site that people will be touring? Can people accidentally wander into your wedding reception? If it's at a park or public building, can it be closed off or at least made clear that a reception is in progress? Thinking about this will help you keep the atmosphere you're hoping for and save you from feeding wandering tourists on their way through.

- **Last, ask yourself,** "Is this the kind of place where my guests would feel comfortable?" Can my elderly relatives make it down to the beach? Is this the kind of place we could have kids around? If it's a beautiful backyard but largely taken up by a giant swimming pool, you may want to ask guests to leave their kids at home, or think of another location. You can't please everyone, but be considerate of those who you really wish would attend. After all, your guests' comfort, next to yours, is most important.

❏ Reserve reception venue

Reserve the venue you have chosen in the previous step. You'll want to do this prior to ordering the invitations so that you can guarantee it before putting the address on three hundred invitations.

❏ Select engagement photo

Choose a picture you both like and that represents you well. However, be considerate to your parents and guests on the appropriateness of the picture you choose. It's a time to put your best foot forward and show your love and commitment more than your silliness.

❑ Print engagement photos

This can be done professionally or through a store such as Kinko's or Walmart. Be sure to double check your selected photo for anything you might not like having three hundred copies of (for example: food in your teeth or a wardrobe malfunction).

❑ Decide reception time

Do you want a late afternoon wedding followed by a dinner reception? It will be best to do this step after scheduling the temple, so as to plan around their sealing openings.

You need to decide not only the time of day but also the length of time for the reception. You want to choose a time that makes it easiest for the majority of your guests to attend. Outside of business hours is a good first policy.

Take into account that you'll be standing for a good part of the reception, as will your parents or anyone else you put in the receiving line. You don't want to go too late, for the sake of those with children and also for ease in cleanup. You do want to allow time to greet all the guests and for the events you expect. And also, don't forget to leave about an hour for pre-reception pictures.

Most guests will not stay longer than two hours. Some may pop in and go right away, and others may stay the full duration. The length of time depends entirely on what you are going for. Sit down and eat? Dancing? Munch and mingle? You'll need plenty of time to greet your guests and at least thirty minutes to do all the cake, garter, bouquet stuff. Two and a half to three hours is about perfect. If you are having a sit-down meal or program, remember to indicate so on your invitations. For instance, Receiving line from 6–7 p.m., dinner and dancing to follow. That way, anyone wishing to reach you in a formal receiving line can plan their arrival accordingly.

chapter five

invitations

❑ **Compile guest lists**
   (Temple guests, luncheon guests, reception guests, and shower guests)

This is one of the most time-consuming tasks. There are several guest lists that need to be thought of and arranged. You will want to have a master guest list by the end that indicates who the guests are, where to mail the invitation to and which events they are invited to. We'll take the lists one at a time, but one general piece of advice that applies to all of them is that you'll want to double and triple check all your lists. Don't try to make any one guest list in one sitting. You'll want to walk away and let it stew while more people come to mind or you rethink the people you've already chosen. And absolutely never make any plans based on someone's off-the-cuff estimate. Also, don't give anyone an off-the-cuff estimate. Don't make any plans until everyone has gone over their family tree and you have actual names. This is not the time for guessing.

Compile detailed lists of actual people for all the events, especially for the temple. Decide if you are going to invite children and, if so, to which events. Make a file or start a notebook. Give yourself an outline with places for each guest's name, address, what they are invited to (such as ceremony, reception, shower), and if they have responded. It is also a good idea to add spots on this list to keep track of if they brought a gift and if a thank you note has been sent already.

Single adult guests over eighteen should be sent their own invitation, even if they live with other people who are also invited (such as siblings, parents, roommates).

Start with everyone you can think of and then back off the list as it becomes too big. Think of singles and determine if you will add an "and guest" to their invitation. You are not obligated to invite a guest for singles.

You may want to prioritize your guest wish list from the beginning, such as family first, then friends, then ward, then coworkers. This will make it easy to trim down later, should you need to. This is a good time to begin collecting the addresses as well, especially if using a computer file. It's just as easy to copy and paste the address with the name, and it will save you a step later.

Tip: Keep this list around after the wedding, as it can be used for future family weddings.

Everyone should make a list: bride, groom, and parents of each. Don't forget to sift through the lists in case of duplicates. You may not have to cut as many as you think. Don't forget to set a deadline for completed lists.

Tip: Remember the best way to cut costs is to cut the guest list. A larger guest list means more invitations and food, and a bigger venue, for starters.

Groom—You have to make a list. Who does? You do. Everyone does. Including who? You. You with me? You need to think of people you like too. Your family and bride will not think of all your old roommates and missionary companions. Not too mention your old bud that melted your sister's Barbie with a magnifying glass with you. Come on. You need these guys.

Bride—It is your job to make sure the groom's family is included. Ask his mother for a list. Talk with her directly. Do not assume your beloved prince charming will think of all the people who are important to his mommy.

Problem: Do I have to invite my whole ward?

The quick and dirty answer is no. Even if you are the bishop. You invite the people you can accommodate and the people you really want there. You don't need to print out the ward list. If you are having an open house and you can accommodate the whole ward as they mingle in and out, then great. However, please don't feel obligated. You don't have to invite anyone you don't want to.

• **Temple guests**—This is the guest list for your ceremony, whether or not you're getting married in the temple. Your choice of guests is a very sensitive subject. You'll want to be careful. The temple provides built in limitations on your guest list. All guests will need to be worthy temple recommend holders. So the most common question is . . . Do I invite someone who can't come to the temple (for whatever reason), because they are very close to me and would be hurt if I didn't even invite them to the ceremony? Now, first of all, you can't possibly know the worthiness of all your potential ceremony guests. The temple encourages you to invite only your closest relatives to your wedding ceremony. This is not supposed to be a cathedral wedding. It's personal and sacred. If you start there, with your most intimate relatives, two things will be a lot simpler. One, you are more likely to know if they are worthy temple recommend holders. Two, they will understand that you can't invite everyone to the temple.

I know you'll want to invite everyone close to you just so they know they're invited, even if you both know they can't come. This is not appropriate. Do not invite them to the ceremony. Invite them to the reception. They will understand and probably already know that they can't possibly come to the temple, so all will be well. The standard for the LDS religion is not set by you but by God, and upheld by the brethren of the Church. Refer to the resources in the back of this book for a link to an *Ensign* article about helping your family understand why they can't come to the temple and to help ease hurt feelings.

You can invite the intimate members of your family who cannot attend the ceremony to come later to the temple to see the bridal couple emerge and to be in the pictures. The temple has a small waiting room just inside the door where supervised children or other guests not attending the ceremony may wait. Don't invite lots of people to wait in this room. It will not be a large room, and it also needs to maintain the peaceful reverence that the temple appreciates. Most temples will allow the sealer to accompany the couple out to the waiting room to answer any questions and help the family understand. You will need to ask the sealer to come outside, as this will not be expected.

President Boyd K. Packer taught:

> The young couple must understand that their parents may have looked forward to the wedding day during the entire lives of the bride and groom. Their desire to attend the wedding, and their resentment when they cannot, is a sign of parental attachment. It is not to be resented by the young couple. It is to be understood and planned for carefully as a part of the wedding. *(Preparing to Enter the Holy Temple.* Salt Lake City: Intellectual Reserve, 2002.)

As far as a number count, count the invitees, not the guests you expect. If you don't expect them, don't invite them. You have a very limited number of seats, and it is not inappropriate to call Aunt Kathryn who lives in Chicago and ask if there's any possibility she'll be flying in for the wedding. If there is a possibility, then you need to count her seat as taken. If she says it's unlikely, then you need to explain to her that you love her and will miss her, but you'll be inviting another guest.

I have seen it happen where the family invited more guests than they had room for thinking that the guests would probably not come. More guests came than were expected and filled the sealing room. When the mother of the bride came into the room after assisting her daughter, she found there was no place for her to sit. She was escorted from the room in tears. Another guest had to leave to allow the mother to see the sealing. You really have only the number of seats that the temple says. Better to have a few empty seats because someone didn't show than to not have room for Mom.

The last thing to take into account when making the temple guest list is a boundary line. There has to be a consistent boundary line for all guests, no matter whose family they're from. For instance, the boundary line could be immediate family. But where is the line, really? What about your stepbrother? Is he invited? What about your sister's husband . . . ? The line should be as simple as possible. You have to clearly define this line and stick to it. Yes, there may be exceptions to the line. If Great-Auntie Dell always sends a card on your birthday and visits regularly, then she should be invited, but it doesn't mean you have to invite your third cousin who you've never met to keep the line perfect. However, anytime you stray from the boundary line, it must be communicated with the groom and his family so they are not offended. The allowance should be made for him and his family to invite such people as well. No matter what your reasons are for varying outside a consistent boundary, your guests will not all understand. You don't get to decide if your guests' feelings are hurt or if they should be offended. This is a place where feelings are very sensitive. So be cautious.

I once attended a civil wedding ceremony that I had been told my children were not invited to. No problem. Totally reasonable to not have children there. Until I got there and saw a child there. I was instantly hurt. Why were my children expressly not invited? Was it something specific about my children? It was explained to me, to placate me, the connection of the child to the bride. This connection happened to be the exact same connection as my children's connection to the groom. So then I was doubly hurt. It totally was my children. I knew it! They hated my poor, sweet, gorgeous children. Then I was mad. I was leaving offended and considered not going to the reception either. This all sounds petty, I know, but you can't always control your feelings. And no feelings get defensive faster then that of a mother hen. I found out later that the boundary line had not been consistent and that a miscommunication had occurred as to the reason for the exclusion. No offense had been intended. Yet because the boundary was so varied and complex, feelings were unintentionally hurt and now, years later, it still stings. That's what I mean when I say to think about your guests' feeling as well. No matter what your reason for the exclusion, it is easiest to assume the exclusion is personal.

Now, the opposite side of this is . . . you can't make everyone happy. You can't please everyone. A line must be set. But if you respect the boundary line, so will your guests.

Last, if you have intimate family members who are unable to attend the sealing ceremony, such as your mom and dad, it is a good idea to keep the guest list very, very small. Don't get a big room and then fill in their spots with other people. Set a line and stick to it and then get a smaller room for the number of guests required. This will help them to feel included instead of feeling as if others are there filling their spots, which says, "everyone gets to come except you."

• **Wedding Luncheon Guests:** This list is usually pretty easy. It's supposed to be everyone who was invited to the temple, plus anyone who still fits within your boundary line that was unable to attend the temple ceremony, such as: younger guests, guests that aren't endowed, non-members, and so on—anyone who would have been invited to the ceremony, should there have been no limitation of a temple recommend. Make sure you invite everyone in the wedding party.

These invitations can be sent separately to cut down on the inserts in the general wedding invitation.

• **Reception Guests:** This is everyone. The big giant list. Everyone. No list will include more people than this one. Did I say everyone? You will never remember everyone the first time through, unless you're my mother and you've been keeping a detailed list of all of the people you know or have known for the entire span of your life. Everyone includes all your extended family. Don't forget to invite all your immediate family. This is also your friends from school, work, your mission, and so on, plus your ward members, your old dance teachers, your mentor, and your coach. Everyone.

Note! The exception to this list being giant is if you are having a small, intimate dinner reception. Then this list will be significantly smaller. But you will still want an all-inclusive, giant list for announcements.

• **Bridal Shower Guests:** I'll go into this in detail in the bridal shower chapter. But it is a good idea to have your bridal shower in mind as you make these lists. It will come in handy later.

❑ Plan accommodations for out-of-town guests

There are many schools of thought on this. Do I have to pay for my out-of-town guests' travel and accommodations? My thought in the gospel of Ann is, no. But you do have to help them out with some planning. Likely the guests are coming to you, so it is reasonable to assume that you would have a better idea of where they could stay. Perhaps they could stay with family members who live nearby. You could help them price hotels.

However, if it's your grandma, and she can't afford to come so you are paying for her, you need to make sure she has a place to stay when she gets here.

Hotel accommodations may be required for the bridal couple and immediate family as well, if they are traveling away from their home to their groom's hometown, or perhaps just to the closest temple. If such is the case, this is just the check box for that. If no travel is needed or the guests traveling do it all the time and so are set, then no problem. It's an easy box to check off, right?

❑ Choose invitations

Announcements versus invitations? Technically, announcements are sent to people to whom you wish to announce your marriage to, but who are not invited to the wedding celebrations. Specifically, far away friends and relatives. We as Mormons tend to send one card that both announces the marriage and invites people to the reception. We then often include a ceremony insert to invite them to this most sacred sealing. If you are having a small reception with not too many guests, you may consider sending announcements to anyone else who may care but isn't invited to the festivities. Announcements are generally sent a day or two after the wedding, whereas invitations are sent well in advance to allow people time to prepare to come.

If you are sending an announcement instead of an invite, simply remove the invitation section in the wording. For instance:

Mr. and Mrs. Ralph Jones
are pleased to announce the marriage of their daughter
Angela
to
Bradley James Smith,
son of Mr. and Mrs. John Smith
on Friday, February twenty-fourth
Two thousand Twelve
in the Salt Lake City Temple.

Invitations can be ordered as a whole or in pieces. Most people create their own invitations now. You can go to a paper store and choose your paper and have it cut, go to a printing company to have them printed, and go to another store to have a photo printed. Many stationery stores will have invitation ideas. If you don't want to create your own, reception centers or wedding planners can generally include invitations as part of their services. You can also easily order invitations online.

Don't forget to order or print ceremony inserts as well. These are generally smaller and are inserted into the envelope of the wedding announcement. Make sure you communicate to all your temple guests that: they need to wear their best Sunday clothes, not their temple whites. Also, they need to bring their current temple recommend and be thirty minutes early. You may also need invitation cards to a ring ceremony or the luncheon to insert in here as well.

The old-fashioned invitation includes a 5 x 7 sheet, printed with the wedding/reception information; a small sheet of tissue paper; a small photo of the couple; and a small ceremony insert. These are enclosed in an inner envelope, followed by an outer envelope. This form is not very common anymore, but it is still my preferred invitation type. However, invitations are as varied as the couples.

Keep in mind special postage. For instance, a square invitation can cost twelve cents more per piece to mail. It is a good idea to find out how much certain invitations will cost. It saves on surprise fees later. Reply cards, inserts, and envelopes all add extra weight to the postage and should be considered as well.

Some things to keep in mind: How easy is the invitation to read? How much will it cost to mail? Is it tasteful? Does it reflect our thoughts about the special nature of this occasion? How annoying will it be to do in bulk? For instance: one small ribbon or gem or stamp can be cute and may not seem very time consuming, until you're doing it to a couple hundred invitations.

❑ Determine invitation wording and layout

The wording can be done in many ways, but there are a few standards:

- the people who are paying for the majority of the wedding— the hosts—put their names first
- use the full, given names of all parties
- don't abbreviate things except Mr., Mrs., Ms., Dr., and Jr.
- capitalize only proper nouns and the first letter of the year (the year should start on a new line)
- all numbers are written out (six o'clock on the evening of Wednesday, the nineteenth of June, Two thousand twelve). Don't put an "and" in the year

Examples

Mr. and Mrs. Tyler Peterson

Ann and Tyler Peterson

Mr. Tyler Peterson

The man's first and last name are never separated, so his name is the one used or that goes last to keep the names together.

You then add the wording of what you are announcing:

are pleased to announce the marriage of their daughter

request the pleasure of your company
at the marriage of their daughter

request the honor of your presence at the
marriage ceremony of their daughter

Note! The reception invitation is generally worded as "the pleasure of your company," and the ceremony invitation is generally worded as "the honour of your presence," but either can be used in either instance.

Generally in LDS weddings we announce the marriage and then state the names of the bride and groom (bride always goes first), followed by the names of the groom's parents, and finish with a request for the "pleasure of your company at a reception held in their honor" or some such wording.

The names of the groom's parents can be announced directly following the groom's name.

son of Mr. and Mrs. Henry Thompson
son of Jane and Henry Thompson

The "son of" can be left off the invitation. You can also start the invitation with "together with their parents" and then put the names of the bride and groom. The parents' names can go at the bottom of the invitation, leaving a space for parents of the bride and parents of the groom. Or if the bride and groom are paying for their own wedding, you can leave the parents' names off and have the wedding announced by the engaged couple themselves. Whichever best suits your family dynamic.

When choosing the wording for your invitations, keep in mind:
- **Clarity**—can everyone understand it?
- **Legibility**—can everyone read it? (Don't use a funky script.)
- **Complete information**—does it have all the necessary information?
- **Flow**—is it disjointed or does it roll off the tongue?

Be sure to put the temple name and address on the ceremony insert to avoid anyone going to the wrong temple.

Example

The honor of your presence is requested at the sealing ceremony at eight o'clock on the morning of Friday, January sixth

Two thousand twelve

at the Salt Lake Temple

50 West North Temple Street

Salt Lake City, UT 84150-9709

Please arrive thirty minutes prior to the ceremony.

One cute idea is "Johnny and Sally are pleased to announce the marriage of their mom, (bride's name), to (groom's name)." I think that's very sweet.

Special circumstances: First—if the parents of the bride or the groom are divorced, the wording will be different. You could put "Mr. John Smith and Mrs. Jane Brown are pleased to announce . . ." or "Mr. and Mrs. John Smith and Mrs. Jane Brown are pleased to announce . . ." or announce the marriage and put the parents of the bride and groom at the bottom of the invitation.

Second—if either parent is deceased, you may add their name by adding "the late" before it. However, do not make a deceased person the first name on the invitation.

Third—if you are having more than one reception, you can print two sets of invitations, each with one reception listed, and then send it to the associated guest. However, the easier and more widely done solution, is to simply print both reception dates, times, and locations on the bottom of all the invitations, and people will attend the one they can.

❏ Determine if RSVPs are needed and order them

If you are having a dinner that needs an exact count, you'll need to send out RSVP cards with self-addressed stamped envelopes to be returned. Open house–type receptions don't require an RSVP. It all really depends on your venue and caterer and what they can accommodate and accomplish within your price range. It is also becoming more and more common, and thus socially acceptable, to have an email they may respond to, or have them log onto your wedding website to mark down their expected attendance. Make sure you set a postmark due date (of two to three weeks before the wedding) on the RSVPs to make sure you have them back in time. You'll need to determine the look and wording of these cards (such as, "Kindly RSVP prior to August 5, 2011") and have them ordered, usually with the invitations.

It is a good idea to have a place on your guest list spreadsheet where you can mark any returned RSVPs. This will help you keep track of who's been invited and who's responded.

If people don't respond, you have two choices. One—contact them and try to get a response. Use the best means available, phone or email, whatever is the best way to reach that person. Two— assume they will be coming. I know it can be difficult and even annoying. Most people will RSVP and, if not, they probably forgot or misplaced their response card. Best to give them the benefit of the doubt. It's better to plan for them and have too much food, than to not plan on them and not have a place for them to sit.

❏ Order wedding invitations

This will need to be done well in advance. Try to get a proof before the whole lot is printed to avoid the need for reprints. You also need to allow plenty of time for addressing them. (You may be able to get your envelopes earlier than your invitations so you can start addressing them. Just make sure they fit the invitations and all the inserts before you go to all the trouble.) Order more than you need, just in case you have any last-minute additions, plus then you get to keep one for your scrapbook!

❏ Prepare a map for invitation, if applicable

If you require a map to find any venue, you'll need to create one. This really is as simple as typing the address into maps.google.com and printing out the directions from a major freeway or some such. Please, oh please, oh please, don't hand draw this map. It can be very hard to decipher if that scribble was a road to turn on or a shake of the hand. We don't want to have to hand out decoder rings with each invitation, now, do we? Oh, and make sure you include the address in case they get lost.

❏ Purchase thank you cards

Thank you cards can be ordered to match the invitations, or they can simply be chosen from a store. Remember to keep them tasteful. The big "Thanks!" cards that you use for an eight-year-old's birthday party may not be appropriate.

❏ ♦ Decide on and order "luncheon" invitations

This is a fine thing to do separate from the wedding invitation, especially since the luncheon is traditionally given by the groom's side of the family. RSVPs tend to be more common for this meal, as it is usually more intimate and dependent on the number of guests.

❏ ♦ Address and mail "luncheon" invitations

These invitations can be sent on their own or added, as an insert, into the wedding invitation.

❏ Find addresses for everyone on guest lists

Addresses—no, not email addresses but real dwelling places—are required. The wedding announcements need to be sent in hard-copy, as the computer-savvy like to call it. It is just plain tacky to email your announcements out. And no, a Facebook invite doesn't count either. I won't even apologize for that.

❑ Address wedding invitations

Traditionally, this should be done using a pen and your hand. I know it's faster and easier to just print your addresses on labels, but it is worth it to take the time. Hand addressing them is much more personal, and it will also give you an opportunity to catch any errors in names or addresses. Just enlist people (like your bridesmaids) to help you so you don't have to do them all yourself. And plan lots of time for addressing these. Even if you're using labels, it takes time to arrange the list, print it, stuff envelopes, address them, and stamp them.

If you decide you want to print them, the best way is to use a script font and to print it directly onto the envelope. Make sure to edit your address spreadsheet so that you print only the names and addresses and that they are formatted correctly: "Mr. and Mrs. Tyler Peterson," and not "Peterson, Ty and Ann." Be careful that the font is legible at different sizes. You can have this done at the print shop or you can do it at home. If doing it at home, use a good quality printer. If you are going to use labels, the best choice is clear—it looks better than the white, even if your envelope is white.

If you're going with my preferred invitation choice, then the outer envelope would say "Mr. and Mrs. Tyler Peterson" and the address. The inner envelope would say, "Tyler, Ann, (and each child's name, if invited)." If you don't know the children's names, you can write, "and children" or "and family" in order to still include them. Rule of etiquette: if the children's names don't appear on the envelope at all, then they are not invited.

✍ **Note!** Don't count on all your guests leaving children at home unless it's been specifically asked of them, using wording such as, "Adults only please" on the invitation.

If you have only an outer envelope, use the most formal name. If the guest is single, it would read, "Miss Sharon Jones" or "Miss Sharon Jones and Guest." If you are printing the addresses instead of handwriting them, you need to take some time in your document and fix them so they read this way as well. It should never say,

"Peterson, Tyler and Ann" because that's the way they appear in your file. Oh, and make sure their name is spelled correctly.

This is also the time to stuff the invitations. Be careful to put the ceremony cards (and any other insert cards) in the correct invitations.

❑ Mail invitations

Take one invitation, complete with all its frills, enclosures, and envelopes, to the post office to check the postage. Many invitations require more than the traditional amount of postage.

Double check that you have the right stamps for mailing, especially any international ones. You can get "wedding motif" stamps for no extra charge at the post office. You should mail the invitations four to eight weeks in advance—if needed, leaving time for an RSVP cutoff date—so you have time for your final count.

❗ Soapbox Warning

Mail the invitations. Don't walk them to my front door. I don't care if I live next door. Also, it's illegal to place anything in a mailbox. Mail it. What? Is my attendance at the reception and the $25 gift I'm going to bring not worth the price of a stamp?

chapter six

ceremony

This list is for a temple ceremony. If you are having a civil ceremony, then all the parts of this section may not apply. Also, special circumstances can arise that require other information, such as, if a temple divorce is needed for this ceremony to continue or if any adoption proceedings are necessary or if you are providing the sealer instead of the temple.

This temple sealing is the reason for the whole day. Starting an eternal family. It is sacred and special. Don't let this most important part of your wedding day get overshadowed by all the party planning and details that will follow. Ask your dad or another worthy priesthood holder for a blessing the night before or morning of your wedding. Give yourself time to soak in the spirit you feel there so it may stay with you throughout the entire day. Let yourself be happy and let it show to all who see you.

❗ Soapbox Warning

A word about the day of the ceremony: You need to be ready (as in hair and make-up, not wearing your dress) when you go to the temple. You are not asked to come early to give you time to get ready. Give yourself plenty of time to get yourself ready at home. I mean a *lot* of time. You don't want to feel rushed and pushed. If it takes you a half hour normally, give yourself at least an hour. You should change into your dress at the temple, but other than that, you need to be ready.

Don't keep your guests waiting at the temple before or after the ceremony. Don't plan to ready yourself again after the ceremony (except to change if need be). People will be waiting on you. It can be rude and selfish of you to make them wait an extended period of time. Just quickly remove the sacred clothing and come straight out. I have literally waited over an hour for the bride to re-emerge after the ceremony, and she looked exactly the same as when I had just seen her. You look beautiful, now get out there.

❏ Get marriage license

(👤 Groom: you pay for the wedding license)

Getting a marriage license is one of the "i's" that has to be dotted or you legally cannot get married. It is a pretty simple process but has to be done by both the bride and groom together.

You will need the following to apply for a marriage license:
- Both parties must be present at the time of application.
- Full names, addresses, and dates and places of birth.
- The social security number of both parties, unless a party doesn't have a social security number.
- The names and birth places of the parents of both parties, including mothers' maiden names.
- Valid picture IDs such as a passport, birth certificate, driver's license, or state ID card.
- In some states you will also need blood tests and full physicals. There are restrictions as to when to get them relative to your application for a marriage license. Look it up on your state website, www.(name or initials of your state).gov and it will tell you.

Apply for a marriage license at any county clerk's office. As soon as you get your license, you can get married. The license is usually valid for 30 days. (Some states' are valid for longer). The license fee is somewhere between $35 and $100 by cash, check, money order, or some credit cards. Check with your local government to verify current cost, payment options, validation times, and if there is an application waiting period.

Many times a license issued in one county may be used in any county within the state. If you are crossing state borders, you need a valid marriage license for the state you are being married in. Check online. Often you can preprint and fill out the application to take with you when you apply.

❏ Choose & ask your ceremony witnesses

The witnesses are often the father of the bride and the father of the groom, but any temple-worthy endowed male can do it. They'll need to arrive early at the temple on your wedding day in order to receive instruction and sign your marriage certificate. If you don't have anyone, the temple will provide someone.

❏ Choose & ask your escort

The bride and groom are each allowed one escort to go to the temple with them. The escort's function is to be a support throughout the temple. A parent is a good choice. The bride's escort will often help the bride into her clothes. It is okay if you don't have an escort; the temple will have sisters and brothers to assist you. Your escort will come to the temple, the same time as you, to help you finish getting ready and assist you throughout the rest of the process. They wear their best Sunday clothes, not their temple whites.

❏ Schedule appointment with bishop and stake president for a living ordinance recommend

✍ **Note!** Both the bride and groom have to do this even if they have a temple recommend and even if they are previously endowed. This, like your marriage license, is necessary in order to get married.

If you don't have your living ordinance recommend with you when you get to the temple, they will not allow you to get married. Obtaining this recommend within that last month is plenty of time, but don't wait too long because you'll need time to meet with the bishop and stake president.

❑ Meet with bishop and stake president to obtain living ordinance recommend

Really, you need the recommend or no wedding.

This checkbox is here for after the meeting is held and the recommend obtained.

❑ Make arrangements for and receive endowments, if needed

If you have not already received your own endowments, this will need to be done prior to your wedding. This is a large thing in and of itself. Your endowments can be done prior to your wedding day, although some couples' circumstances require that this be done on the same day. If you have the time to spare, I would recommend not doing it on your wedding day; because this is a very special and wonderful thing, you should give yourself time to absorb the endowment before the wedding. It's a truly amazing and spiritual experience, and it would be nice to let it simmer before rushing back into the wedding preparations.

Getting your endowments requires its own recommend and preparations. Check with the temple. They have special sessions for "live" endowments, and you'll need to schedule accordingly.

You will be allowed to bring one escort (your same gender) for your live endowment. This can be anyone endowed and temple worthy. Your escort will be with you all the time, helping and instructing. If you do not have an escort, the temple can provide one.

If you are the bride getting your endowments for the first time, your groom needs to come, and other guests may attend as well. If you are the groom getting your endowments, your bride doesn't need to come, but may be invited. You may invite other guests as well. The session will be open to other temple patrons in addition to your guests.

You should wear your Sunday dress to the temple, and there you will change into your white temple dress, which can be purchased, borrowed, made, or rented. You will need to bring a pair of clean, never-before-worn temple garments with you that you will put on during a short initiatory session prior to your endowment. I recommend buying a few pairs of garments at first, then filling in your supply later after you see how you like the fit and material.

You will also need what is sometimes called a "packet" or your "sacred clothing." This packet can be purchased at a church distribution center. Larger temples will have clothing rentals available, but check with the temple to be sure, as some temples don't have a laundry facility and so don't rent clothing.

You will need a living ordinance recommend for your endowment—separate from your sealing recommend. This will require interviews with your bishop and stake president. You may be advised by them to attend a temple preparation class.

❏ Make arrangements for "day of" transportation

This is just for the bride and groom and can easily be overlooked. You'll first want to decide how each of you is going to get to the ceremony. I personally rode in the same car as my groom just so I knew we'd get there on time and to the right place, and if not, at least we'd be together.

You'll also want to think about the rest of your schedule for the day. Remember, you'll be married now and will want to ride in the same car. You'll need transportation to the luncheon, the reception, and the hotel for the night, as well as to any other place you may need to go, such as a place to rest in the middle of the day.

When thinking of the ride away from the reception to the wedding night location, sometimes people like to do something out of the ordinary. That's okay; but make sure that if you hire anyone (such as a limo, carriage, or private jet), don't keep the driver waiting. It may cost extra. Ask the company if the fee is hourly or a flat rate. Give them a pickup time and place to be and be ready at that time at that place. Also, keep in mind what you'll be wearing. Some vehicles can be harder or dirtier to get in and out of if you're in your wedding dress.

If you're driving your own car, it might be a good time to think about how you feel about your car being decorated. If you don't mind, then leave it parked where you will. If you really want your car left alone, you might want to communicate that to your family and wedding party. If you're still nervous about it being tampered with, have it parked off location and have a trusted friend or family member go retrieve it right before you're ready to leave. (Refer to chapter fifteen for more on decorating the car.)

❏ Pack for temple trip
❏ Bring rings to temple

I'm grouping these together because they are both packing for the temple. The reason I have them in separate checkboxes on the list is because people tend to forget the rings since they aren't part of the ceremony. Following the ceremony, the sealer will give the couple the opportunity to exchange rings in the sealing room.

The night before, double check that you've packed everything. Many a couple have arrived at the temple without their marriage license.

Since I'm a list person—if you haven't noticed, and make lists for my lists—here's a general temple packing list. Refer to appendix D for a full emergency bride kit. You should go to the temple wearing your regular best Sunday clothes. That is why the wedding dress and groom's tux appear on this list.

- marriage license
- CURRENT temple recommend (for ALL people attending the temple ceremony. Mom—Don't forget yours!)
- living ordinance recommend (both bride and groom: even if you're previously endowed!)
- wedding rings
- temple packet
- temple shoes
- wedding dress or temple dress
- wedding dress underclothes (slip, corset, stockings)
- wedding veil
- touch-up makeup (including toothbrush)

- touch-up hair supplies
- small sewing kit
- groom's ordinance clothes
- groom's tux or suit (as he'll have to change for pictures)

❑ Iron temple packet

If you think about how much time is spent making sure all your "civil" wedding clothes look just perfect, it's not much to ask to prepare the sacred clothing as well. I've found that ironing your packet before heading off to the big day is a small task that will make a nice difference.

❑ Finalize your "day of" schedule

You need to finalize your wedding day schedule at least a week before the wedding. Think through each aspect and make sure everything is on the schedule, including times and addresses.

❑ Make sure all immediate family members have a "day of" schedule

You'll want to give a "day of" schedule to the entire wedding party. Include details such as which temple and all specific addresses. (We don't want people going to the wrong temple.) Then there is no miscommunication of when anyone is supposed to be where. It will help them all get a full plan and will make sure they all got the memo.

Tip: It is also a good idea to give this schedule to all your venders or helpers so they can be in on the full plan as well.

chapter seven

ring ceremony

Exchanging rings is not a part of the temple ceremony. Some couples exchange rings after the ceremony in the sealing room. A ring ceremony is a separate ceremony that some couples elect to have after the temple sealing and at a different time and location. This is not required and not necessary. The temple sealing is a complete wedding ceremony. However, since you must be not only LDS but also endowed and temple worthy to attend the temple sealing, many couples have a ring ceremony to include their parents or other family members who cannot be at the temple.

❑ Determine whether to have a ring ceremony

❑ Determine how ring ceremony will be presented

There are guidelines to such a ceremony, and they may change. It is best to check with your bishop to make sure you are following the current rules.

The basic guidelines are as follows:
- it should not take place on the temple grounds
- it should remain respectful of the temple marriage
- it should not mimic or replicate any part of the temple marriage ceremony
- the couple should not exchange vows

Other than that, it's pretty open. I myself would keep the ring ceremony simple and intimate. I wouldn't want people to think that the temple ceremony is incomplete, so I wouldn't have any of the "normal" civil ceremony things. We should make it clear to our guests that the couple is already married.

! Soapbox Warning

If you must have a ring ceremony, it should not be bigger than the temple ceremony. It should not overshadow or replace the temple ceremony. Some people add extra flowers, music, programs, attire, and so on to make this another big ceremony, and it really shouldn't be. If you are going to do it, it should be simple and low-key and it should be emphasized that the couple is married already and that the ring ceremony is extra. Don't have an aisle and a ring bearer and "Here Comes the Bride." The temple is the wedding.

❏ Choose a place for the ring ceremony

It is a good idea to have the ring ceremony in a different room than the reception. Then the reception can stay set up and no change-over is necessary.

❏ Determine a time for the ring ceremony

Right before the reception or the pictures at the reception is best. Then the guests can go straight from the ceremony into the reception or straight to the pictures. This will also help to have every-one already gathered.

❏ Determine who will conduct the ring ceremony

Since this ceremony is not a legality or an ordinance, anyone can conduct. I would choose the bishop or one of the fathers of the engaged couple.

It is a good idea to ask this person to spend three to five minutes talking about the importance of eternal marriage.

chapter eight
wedding luncheon

The groom's side traditionally handles the "luncheon." The luncheon can be as simple or as extravagant as you decide to make it. It could be a potluck meal in your home or a catered event complete with place cards, speeches, and a program. So hike up your stockings and dive in or let your hair down and relax. Is that enough clichés? Just calm the heck down. It'll be okay. You'll need to consider a few things in making your decisions about the luncheon. Why are you having it? When will you have it? Where will you have it? How will you handle the food? Will there be any entertainment? Do you need to do any decorating? Deep breaths. One step at a time.

Note! Depending on when you have it, you may be coming straight from the ceremony yourself. If so, don't plan for you or any of the wedding party to do any of the work at the luncheon.

Why are you having it? The wedding luncheon has come to be the bride and groom's first meal together. It is a bit of a celebration of this. We, as Latter-day Saints, don't have a need for a rehearsal dinner; however, you may prefer to have one the night before. This can be a time for the wedding party to be together to celebrate in a more informal setting than the reception itself. The addition of speeches, a program, a couple video, and so on can make it a lot of fun but aren't necessary. The point is, it is a time of fun and should be fairly intimate, low-key, and relaxing.

❑ Choose a time for the luncheon (if not previously done)

When will you have it? As previously stated, you can have this the night before the wedding. If done on the day of the wedding, the luncheon is usually between the wedding ceremony and the reception. It could be a breakfast or dinner. In this case, it usually follows fairly soon after the ceremony. Make sure to give time for the bride and groom to take pictures at the temple and change their clothes and for all the guests to travel to the luncheon venue. Then plan on the luncheon being an hour and a half to two hours long. For instance: if the wedding is at 9:30 a.m., plan on pictures from 10:30 to 11:30 a.m. Then start the luncheon between noon and 12:30, depending on how far the guests have to travel.

One benefit to having this meal the night before the wedding is that it's more relaxed. It also opens up time for the bride and groom on the wedding day, so they won't be so rushed.

❑ Choose a luncheon venue (if not previously done)

Where will you have it? The simplest method is to go to a restaurant. Most of them have a banquet room that they will ready for you and handle all the food prep, service, and cleanup. It is not necessarily the cheapest method. If using a restaurant, then the next several questions get addressed and decided pretty much when you choose the venue. You can read ahead the next few checkboxes for further advice before making this choice.

There are many options. You could do the luncheon at a home, ward house, backyard, or clubhouse, to name a few. I went to one recently in the Relief Society room of a different church than the reception was in. It had been decorated, complete with linens and centerpieces. They had a head table for the bridal couple and their parents and two other long tables for the guests. They brought a caterer in, who provided a beautiful buffet spread. It was really wonderful.

It's really up to you and how much work, time, and money you want to put into it. Be careful though. Don't have it in the same room as the reception unless it is a professional reception hall and they have the means to clean it up and a full staff to then set up the reception. Otherwise it will not be a joyful time, just a crazy time of trying to get people to move along because you need to clear it away for the reception. It will put your guests out and be overwhelming for you.

❏ Prepare and send luncheon invitations (if not previously done)

This may have been done back when you were working on wedding invitations; but if not, it should be done now. Don't assume people will know whether or not they are invited to the luncheon. Send out an invitation. This will help make it clear to everyone that they are, in fact, invited and when and where it is.

❏ Determine who will prepare, serve, and clean up the food

Option A: If you decide to use a restaurant, then you can choose sit-down or buffet. You could, for instance, take everyone to a nice steakhouse and choose a meal for the whole party or have them choose their own meal or even have a select menu to choose from. Or you could pay everyone's entrance into a nice buffet and reserve the banquet room for you all to gather in. (Don't forget to add gratuity into your budget, it adds up for a large party.)

Option Everything Else: If you are not using a restaurant, you have many other options. You can use a caterer. The benefit here is that the caterer will handle the details. You choose a menu and pay them, and they handle the rest. (Make sure you know specifically what "the rest" includes.) You could also ask your friends or neighbors to play caterer or simply make the food yourself. Some people like to have their Relief Society friends make the luncheon and have it ready when the newlyweds and guests arrive. These are all very fine options. But make sure they know that they are preparing it, serving it, and cleaning it up.

❏ Choose a serving style & menu

Again, this can be as big or small a deal as you want it to be. Do you want a buffet or a sit-down-and-be-served meal? Do you want multiple courses? This will be easily decided, if not already decided, should you be using a restaurant. If using a caterer, they will have valuable input into this decision. Different foods work better depending on the way you are eating it. If it's a buffet, you'll need to make sure you can keep foods warm or cold should they need to be. Really, you can do anything from a cold sandwich bar with chips and a veggie tray to a four course meal complete with a garden salad, creamy soup, filet mignon, and a beautifully garnished dessert. Whatever you're willing to work for (or pay for).

❏ Determine which dishes will be used & how they will get there

If using a restaurant, this is a no-brainer. Check! If using a caterer, you'll want to find out if they include dishes in the price. Some don't but will bring dishes for an added fee. If handling the food yourself or with your friends and family, you'll need to arrange for dishes. You may choose to use the ward's dishes. They can often be borrowed even if not using the ward house. You may use your own or a family member's dishes, perhaps their large Thanksgiving guest set. You can always rent dishes, and it is certainly fine and easy to purchase disposable ones.

❏ Purchase food (if not done by professional)

This simply means obtaining the food for the preselected menu should you be handling that yourself.

❏ Determine how decorations will be done

Do you need to do any decorating? This will depend on your venue. You may not need to at all, or it may not be appropriate. If you are decorating or even just setting up tables, someone will need to be assigned to make sure it gets done.

Start with the tables. If you're able to influence how the tables are set up, you'll need a layout plan. Then choose tablecloths, centerpieces, and napkins. Do you want flowers or candles down the center? Maybe beads or confetti? If you want to, then go all out. (You could even do seating arrangements and place cards!) If not, then don't. Don't fret; the luncheon police won't come and get you.

Move on from there to the room. Do you care? Do you want more decorations? Do you want pictures of the couple placed around? Maybe small pillars with candles and flowers. Are you trying to integrate a theme? Determine what you'd like and set about making it happen. Remember, it doesn't have to cost a fortune. You'd be surprised what you can accomplish with some tablecloths over a few small tables and boxes, some white Christmas lights, and a few knick knack objects from your home. Use your imagination.

❑ Determine how entertainment will be handled

Will there be entertainment? This is totally not necessary. You can just have a simple meal together as a new family and visit. But if you'd like, you can arrange for speeches to be made or silly stories about the bridal couple to be told or even their courtship story told. You could have musical numbers or skits. My cousin's dinner had a great program where the mother and brother of the groom wrote a variety radio show that they performed live to tell the couple's courtship. It had several clips from music over the ages for things like, "the first time they saw one another" and "their first kiss." It was so fun to get to know the personalities of this new family joining ours.

If you don't want to go to a lot of effort, you could ask each person to introduce themselves and how they met or know the couple. Or you could simply have soft music playing in the background. The luncheon etiquette is very laid back as to what is required. Mostly, there should be food. I mean, people just expect it if you call it a luncheon . . . I'm thinking. No, really. Just take it from there.

Tip: No matter when you are having your "luncheon," make sure that you and your sweetie eat and drink throughout the day. Stay hydrated.

chapter nine

photography

❑ Select a photographer

Pictures are a very important part of your wedding. These are the only thing tangible you'll have for years to come. I would strongly recommend not using a friend and definitely not a person in the wedding party as the photographer. If you use a member of your family, especially part of the wedding party, they will be busy and not get as many photos as you would like. They would also tend to take more pictures of people they know, whereas a "stranger" photographer would get shots of everyone. I have several friends who, because they used a friend as a photographer, don't have any pictures of their family because the friend took pictures of just the groom's family and his friends.

The main reason for not using a friend or family member is in case they mess up. See, if your friend messed up the cake or the flowers, it might frustrate you, but it wouldn't completely ruin the day, just that aspect. If the photography was bad or ruined, it would be days, or perhaps weeks before you knew. No one could run out and quickly fix it. You would simply have no pictures of a once-in-a-lifetime event. This is one thing that is way worth the money.

Shop around for a photographer. Try both wedding and nonwedding photographers. Look at their work. They should be very willing to show you examples of the caliber of their work, their variety of styles, and the versatility of their vision. Ask them what is included in the price, especially the temple and the reception. Be careful about hidden costs. It is often best to choose the smallest photo package that includes all your must-haves, then make sure you can get additional copies made later (like, should your mom want one.)

Ask them:

• how soon should you expect the photos back?
• how long will it take at the temple? (So you can plan a time for the luncheon. It shouldn't be more than an hour.)
• how early do you need to be at the reception for photos? (So you can plan for that as well as alert the wedding party. It will probably be at least an hour.)
• can they take candid shots as well as posed shots?
• what about their copyright policy?
• how long will they keep the negatives or digital originals?
• if a deposit is required, how much and when?
• total cost (get it in writing) and payment due date?
• what are their cancellation and refund policies?

Also, see how amenable they are to suggested shots that you'd especially like. I really suggest you get the one you want, not the cheapest. After all, this is the biggest thing that will follow you through the years and generations—pictures.

Most important, you should choose a photographer that you and your groom feel comfortable and relaxed with.

❑ Schedule photographer for wedding day

This step is hiring the photographer that you have selected. Remember to schedule him for all the previously described portions of the wedding day. Cameras and photos are not allowed in the temple, so be sure to work out the timing for your photographer to be to the temple as you exit.

Remember the photographer works for you. He is not in charge. Set a time limit, if one hasn't been previously suggested. Some couples have actually been late to their reception because the photographer was calling the shots (pun intended) and insisted on going overtime to get even more pictures.

You are in charge, not them. If you want a specific picture done, you should get it. But remember, there is a reason you chose to use a professional, and one reason is for his experience and expertise. Don't let that go to waste.

❑ Meet with photographer to discuss shots

Let your photographer know some of the shots you are hoping for. Let him know how important the temple is for your photos. He may not realize the strong importance of what the building represents to you. Do you want your shots candid or more posed and formal? Talk about artsy fartsy ones but make sure to ask him for at least one conventional "normal" shot. One that can be passed down to the grandkids.

It is a good idea at photo shoots to start with the biggest group and work your way down. Do everyone in attendance, then one full side of the family (for example, the groom's) then just the groom and his siblings, then him and his mom and dad. Get the picture? No pun intended. Then you can send people away as you finish with them.

Last-Minute Fix-Its

Late sibling? If a member of the wedding party is late, start without him. Do the pictures that he isn't in. Start with the other side of the family. This will give him the most time available to get there but not waste everyone else's time.

Fussy kids? My attitude toward pictures is that they are there to tell a story. If kids are not smiling or what-not, they're still mostly cute. Don't let it ruin your day. The picture that you're going to display most prominently is the one of just you and your sweetie anyway. Don't stress over not being able to wrangle all the children into smiles on the same take. It tells a story.

My wedding reception was a fairly formal affair with my hubby and the dads in tuxes, all the other men in suits, and the women all in nice dresses. My color was yellow, and everyone had kindly accommodated me by dressing to match. We were doing pictures right before the reception, when in walks my brother-in-law. He was wearing shorts. I don't remember who, but someone pointed this out to me. I remember looking over at him, and sure enough there he was in February in Utah in shorts. I remember thinking, "He wore yellow!" I was so excited that he would do that for me. I love that I have a picture of my whole family at my reception in formal attire and him in shorts. It's so him. It reflects who he really is.

I know there is a line. You hope everyone will not take your wedding as a reason to demonstrate themselves in all their glory. But let's face it, can you really stop them? Don't worry. You're still married.

❑ Schedule bridal shoot (if desired)

If you need a bridal shoot, you'll want to check with the photographer to see if it's included in the fee. Then go ahead and schedule it.

! Soapbox Warning

I do not like bridal shoots. I do not like the idea that the whole wedding is about the bride only. It's about both the bride and the groom. In fact, it's not even about the wedding; it's about the marriage. A joyful marriage should not be focused on only one of the individuals. It's supposed to be about both of you working together to create a loving family.

If you want some pictures of the bride in the dress, this can be done individually at the temple or at the reception. You could even take a picture of the groom by himself in his tux. I'll bet he'll look handsome as well.

I do think it's a fun idea to have a previous shoot together with your groom and then have some of your shots finished and displayed at the reception or luncheon. You could go to one of your favorite spots to be together, perhaps even where he proposed.

❑ Have bridal shoot (if applicable)

Go through with the bridal shoot you have previously scheduled.

❑ Ask someone to assist photographer

Let me make it clear that this person is not to bug the photographer all night—after all, you want the photographer to pay attention to taking photos. Just have someone who knows what you want for the shots. They could gather people for the poses and point out family members who aren't part of the wedding party like Great-Aunt Mary.

Idea: Some people use disposable cameras on the tables for the guests to take pictures. These cameras use what is a rare thing nowadays. It's called film. No USB or memory card. You can't plug it in and download it. Ask your grandma what to do. Don't worry. Take this camera to Walmart when you're done; they'll know what to do with it. I know this can end up with some wasted pictures, but you'll be surprised sometimes by what people will catch for you. They take pictures of each other at the tables, and maybe even get sweet ones of you making eyes at your hunky hubby.

❑ Decide how you'll share other candid shots

In this day and age, every other person is carrying a camera, especially with all the latest cell phones. It is a good idea to find a way to ask people for any candid shots they may take throughout the day. I like the idea of having a tech-savvy friend set up somewhere at the reception. Give him a nice table, laptop, and a sign that says, "Share photos of the couple's special day" or some such thing. Have a way to read cards from cameras and an email address to send pictures to. For extra convenience, provide a wifi hotspot so people can send the pictures without using their mobile data plan.

chapter ten

videography

You may use a videographer. Although this is not necessary, it does add one more way to preserve that day. I'll put out the checkboxes for it, but the explanations are pretty much the same as for the photographer. Please refer to the previous chapter for details as to what to consider.

I will, however, add that as opposed to photography, where I strongly recommend using a professional, the video can be done by an amateur. Now, take into account that if you use an amateur, it will not be the same. Videographers know how to work the angles and the lights, and they have ideas about what will fall in place. However, if you are on a tight budget, this is one place that you can save. You could have someone who is great with a camera video as much as possible. Then it can be compiled later with music and a good software program to be a nice video. Again, not the same quality as a professional, but it could still be very nice.

❑ Select a videographer

Again, please refer to the previous chapter for more details, but shop around. Decide if you are going to hire a professional or use a friend. Get a clear picture of what is included in the price and beware of hidden fees. Look at some of their work, and ask how long it will be before you have a finished product in hand. Talk about how things would go on the day of the wedding and find out how much say you get in things like footage, effects, music, and what will be done with any unused material.

❏ Schedule a videographer

After you have selected one, make sure he is are available and schedule him. Make sure you make it clear which portions of the wedding they are attending. For instance, don't come for the sealing ceremony, but come to the reception.

❏ Meet with videographer to discuss shots

You will want to do this whether using a professional or a friend. Let him know how important the temple is to you, if you are having him come to the temple grounds at all. Let him know if you want the cake cutting, speeches, bouquet throwing, couple departure, and so on recorded. Decide if you want him to talk to people to get advice or interviews or if you just want pictures which can be set to music later. Ask him to try to get a variety of people, not just one side of the family, for instance.

chapter eleven

rings

☐ ⚊ Purchase bride's engagement
ring/wedding band set

This is sometimes done by the groom before the engagement is
official, whereas others go ring shopping together. It is a good idea to
have it done before the engagement pictures, as people often view the
ring through them. Also, if only an engagement band was purchased
and a wedding band is desired, you'll need to get that.

Think carefully about where you go for the ring. Choose a repu-
table jewelry store that has been in business for a while. Ask if they
will replace a lost diamond or fix a ring purchased from their store
for free. Many of them will.

When going to choose a ring, you'll need to know a few things.
The sales people will talk to you about the four C's (cut, clarity, color,
and carat) You'll need at least an idea of what cut (meaning which
shape) and carat (meaning how big) you are looking for. These will
narrow down the options for you. If you are buying the ring without
your bride, find out what she likes. Ask her mom, her sisters, her best
friend. Believe me, if anyone knows, they will. The sales person will
ask you many things, such as: gold or white gold, silver or platinum,
solitary diamond or multiple settings.

If you are going together to choose the ring, it's a good idea to
tell your bride up front what your price range is; then she won't be

disappointed that she can't have a bigger ring, and you won't feel obligated to pay more than you can afford to make her happy.

It is becoming more common for the groom to purchase a "staging" ring to use for the proposal and for the couple to go back to the jewelry store later to choose a ring together. That way the groom can still surprise her with a ring, and she still gets to pick out the ring she wants. Girls—if he picks out a ring for you, be kind. It comes with love; and if you get to pick out your own ring, just be sensible. It doesn't need to cost a fortune.

You may need to leave the ring at the jewelry store to have it sized. If you are going to have it engraved, this is a good time to do that as well. Many couples don't have their rings engraved; but if you like, you could choose a special message, your wedding date, or your two initials. It could even say "time and eternity" or "together forever." Keep it on the short side, though, as too many characters won't fit. If you're going to do an engraving, just choose something that best suits the two of you.

❑ Purchase groom's ring

The groom doesn't need a ring, but they are very common. The groom normally chooses his own ring, but you can do whatever works for the two of you. You'll just want to get the ring chosen and purchased.

As with the bride's ring, you may need to leave it to be sized and engraved. This may take a week or two, so leave plenty of time.

❑ Pick up rings from sizing/engraving

Don't forget to pick up the rings and bring them to the temple or the ring ceremony on the wedding day. The jewelry store will tell you when to expect them to be done.

Generally the bride picks up the groom's ring and the groom picks up the bride's ring.

chapter twelve

wedding dress

☐ **Select wedding gown**

Decide what kind of dress you'd like—short or long sleeve; drop waist or empire; train or not; pouffy or straight line; corset torso; square, round, V, or sweetheart neckline; gloves, veil, and so on. Choose a style of dress that complements your coloring, shape, size, and height.

What if you just want to wear your temple dress at the sealing? You don't have to wear a wedding dress at the sealing. You may choose to wear your own temple dress or one the temple provides.

Be careful of color. To get married in the temple, it must be white, not eggshell, ecru, or mother of pearl. White. Hold it up to a sheet of standard computer paper. Now that's white. It can't have an accent color, nor can it use a colored slip inside the temple. It must be floor length, without any slits showing your legs. There are also other standards to be temple ready. The temples try to be consistent with one another, but this is under the jurisdiction of the matron of each temple. You may still get turned away. It is best to refer to your own temple letter for your temple's guidelines.

As an example—the dress guidelines for the Salt Lake Temple in Utah say the dress should be pure white, not off-white, ivory, or cream colored. Some silk fabrics are not white. This may mean you can't wear your mom's dress because it's yellowed. It cannot have elaborate ornamentation or decoration. Everything on the dress must be pure white, including ribbons or embroidery—no silver-backed beads or rhinestones, and be careful with iridescent sequins. It has to be long sleeved (the temple has sleeve inserts), but even short sleeves must cover the unaltered temple garment. Sheer sleeves do not qualify as long. It must have a modest neckline. Be modest in design (so not too tight, ladies) and fabric. Sheer fabric must be lined. If it has a train, the train must be bustled up or removed for the ceremony. You must have all white underclothing (you can't even have a cream bra or nude nylons). *It has to be white.*

The best thing to do is keep the temple in your mind through the whole decision process. Just keep thinking, "Is this temple worthy?" Even if you are not wearing your gown for the ceremony, you should always make sure it modestly covers your garments. Don't think, "I think that might cover my garments." It must. If you're not endowed yet, ask an endowed woman for her advice. Remember, you alter the dress, not the garments. And yes, pinning counts as altering.

A few other things to think about when choosing your dress:

• does it suit my personality and style? (you want your groom to recognize you, right?)

• is my dress appropriate for my location and expected weather—are you dragging a white train across a barn floor, fresh cut grass, or muddy ground? Just think about it. Better to be prepared than sad.

• budget—don't even go looking for a dress you'll never be able to afford. It can only end in tears.

• clearly specify to the sales reps what conditions you are operating under. (If you aren't sure what styles you want, then start by telling them the temple guidelines. You'd be amazed at how many that will sort out.) This will make the dress shopping a lot more fun, as they don't waste your time with dresses you can't use.

❑ Purchase/rent/sew/acquire wedding gown

Think through your timetable before you acquire your dress. Do you plan on losing weight before the big day? You may want to put off the purchase of a dress. If the wedding is a year away, you may not want to buy a tight dress that, should you gain any weight, will suddenly be a very expensive throw blanket.

Determine how you want to obtain your wedding dress, and do so. There are many options: purchase, rent, sew, or borrow.

Purchase

The benefit here is that anything can be bought. So you can get anything and exactly what you want, for a price. The downside is it could be a very large price. Then you are stuck with a dress that you'll never wear again and will yellow in time unless properly sealed, which is also costly. Also, remember you'll need to purchase a veil and underclothes (including a slip, corset, or bustier) and possibly alterations. If you purchase your dress, you may want to also think about gown preservation after the wedding, to keep your gown protected from critters and yellowing.

Try shops that specialize in LDS or modest gowns. Take a day trip to a neighboring city, if need be. You can always do an Internet search for the closest options available. If such a store is not within reasonable geographical reach, then start each visit to the dress shops with a clear description to the sales associate of your modesty requirements. This will speed things along and help her to only bring you options that are actually viable.

Before you purchase, ask the store about deposits required, exchange and refund policies, alteration fees, and how they'll handle any problems that arise.

Rent

The benefit here is that you still have several choices. You are also able to return the dress after the wedding, so you won't have to store it. Check prices against each other, as always. As you're checking prices, ask if the veil and underclothes are included with the dress. Will they alter the dress for you? At what cost? Do you have to have it cleaned, or will the rental company take care of that? How long do you get the dress for? When adding all these things up, sometimes it may be the same as buying, so price it out. If you decide to rent, arrange to pick it up and have someone return it for you while you're on your honeymoon.

As with purchasing, try shops that specialize in modest gowns. This will cut down on the disappointment of not finding an appropriate cut and increase the variety you have to choose from.

Sew

If you can do it, go for it. This will cut down on a need for alterations as the dress will be sewn to fit you. If you are sewing just to save money, it may actually be the same price as buying a simple gown. Plus, then you wouldn't have the added stress of sewing. However, if what you want is simple or totally doable and you love to sew—or your aunt does or your mom does, or you have a very talented acquaintance who does—then do it. It's your dress.

Keep in mind that you may be able to buy an unaltered dress and have that talented seamstress alter it for you, instead of starting from scratch.

Borrow

Borrowing a dress is another totally acceptable alternative, especially if someone else spent a fortune on their dress, and now it's just sitting around. Think it all the way through, though. Their dress may need to be altered, which if it's okay with them, will probably still be cheaper for you than buying your own. Also, who keeps the dress? (They probably should.) And who cleans it? (You should.) And who pays to put it back in preservation, if it had to be taken out? (You probably should.) Also, what if it's chemically preserved and you take it out, then don't use it, who pays for the return to the chemical preservation? (You should.) By the way, a chemical preservation of a wedding dress costs about $200.

Tip: Short on dress budget? Try buying a simple white dress and adding some lace, white embroidery or a white sash. Remember you can always wear your temple dress.

❑ Select and acquire headpiece

You must be able to add and remove your headpiece without changing your hair. So, it can't be braided into your hair. You won't be able to use it in the temple. You'll want to think a bit about how you want your hair when you pick your headpiece. You can wear a veil, a hat, flowers, a wreath, bows, or jewelry. The options are wide. As with your dress, you may buy, rent, sew, or borrow whatever you choose. But if you buy a dress, you don't have to buy a veil. You can mix it up or even not have a headpiece. For instance, you can rent a dress but wear your mom's veil. Just make sure that it complements the style of the dress.

❏ Select and acquire accessories

This includes all accessories: hair pieces, pins, clips, (which remember, need to be removable for the temple), necklace, bracelets, earrings, rings, watch, anklet, gloves, and the list goes on. Just decide what you want and get it, so you have it all ready for the wedding day. Remember that the accessories should complement your ensemble, not overshadow it.

❏ Select and acquire shoes

Choose your shoes carefully. You want them to be cute, but you'll be standing in them all day long. Make sure they are comfortable and supportive if possible. I've seen many a girl wear her favorite tennis shoes under her long dress. No one knew and she was more than comfortable. If you buy new shoes for the wedding, don't forget to break them in. You don't want blisters on your honeymoon. Don't forget to take your wedding shoes to your dress fittings so your gown can be adjusted to the right length.

❏ Plan for the weather

If you are having your wedding in the cold months of the year, you'll want to know if you're just going to wear your regular coat, your dress coat, or a special wrap for just this occasion. Most brides opt out of a coat, even though it's freezing, just so you can see the dress in the pictures. It sounds crazy, I know, but I'm one of those brides, and I was not going to let a cold day ruin all that work and money that had gone into making me beautiful for that day. What we do for fashion, eh ladies?

If it's going to be hot, you may want a parasol or a small fan. If it's rainy, consider a large umbrella that you can both fit under. Just think about how the weather may impact your comfort.

❑ Acquire undergarments

If you buy or rent your dress, a corset, bustier, or slip are sometimes included. However, they may only be included for an added fee. You'll also need nylons and, of course, garments. Gather them and make sure you try them all on. (Don't try on the garments until after you have been endowed.)

❑ Have dress altered and temple ready

Dress size is a touchy subject for most women, yours truly included. But be cautious when determining yours. Be honest with the sales associate and with yourself about your dress size. No one needs to know. You don't want to be squeezed into an uncomfortable dress the whole day. Finding something in your true size will always be more flattering anyway.

You may not need alterations, but it's common enough that it requires a checkbox. You will need a few fittings if you are doing alterations to make sure that everything was altered correctly. Remember, you alter the dress to accommodate the garments, you don't alter the garments to accommodate the dress. Wear the underclothes and shoes to the fitting that you plan on wearing at the wedding. If you haven't been endowed yet, wear underclothing that closely matches that of the garment, to ensure that it will work out well.

If you don't need alterations, it is still a good idea to have a few fittings. This will ensure that nothing has changed or needs to be changed.

One last tip: think about how you want the hemline to be. Do you want your dress to drag on the ground? What if it's snowing the whole day? Just think about your comfort and about how beautiful the dress will look after a day of wearing it through your intended activities. This will help you decide which length best suits you. An inch or two above the ground still constitutes floor length. And don't forget to take into account your shoes and any height they might add.

❑ Purchase garter

This is not necessary, but it is a fun tradition. The garter will need to be purchased, not borrowed, as it will be thrown at the reception. I would probably not wear this all day, but just put it on for the reception.

❑ Have your hair cut or dyed, if desired

I wouldn't do this if you aren't the kind who typically gets this done regularly. But let's face it, most women get it done pretty regularly, right? So, get your hair done well before the wedding—at least a couple of weeks, although it does depend on how fast your own hair grows out. But this isn't the step you want to hold off until the day before the wedding, with no time left to fix any problems that may occur.

❑ Practice doing hair with veil

I mentioned before that you shouldn't weave your veil into your hair. The temple will not allow this. You also cannot have beads, flowers, or ribbon woven into your hair. No ornamentation of any kind can be in your hair, including decorated bobby pins, combs, or claw clips. They will make you take it down, and that will not be without tears. You'll need something that is simple enough that you can switch veils and will look beautiful with both. You don't want to keep your guests waiting outside the temple, because you have to totally redo your hair.

It is a good idea to try your "practice hairdo" for a day. This will show you how you like it, how it weathers the day long, and whether or not it gives you a headache or generally drives you nuts. That way, you won't be stuck with it bugging you on your wedding day.

There are so many options for different hairdos. Try an Internet search for ideas. You could braid, twist, curl, straighten, bun, sweep up, or let loose to name a few. Do something that makes you feel beautiful but still makes you feel like you.

Many brides like to have their nails or hair professionally done for their wedding. This can be fun but is an added and unnecessary expense. Remember that your groom fell in love with you as you are. I know you want to look nice for your wedding, but you do still want to look like you, right? I know your groom hopes you'll look like you.

It could also be fun to practice your makeup. Try out that new lipstick you bought.

If you are going to have your hair styled by someone else, then you'll need to schedule that with them and then make sure you get there to do it the day of the wedding. If they are a professional, then I'd probably just trust that it'll be okay. But if my sister is doing my hair, I'd probably have a practice session.

❑ Have a final wedding dress fitting

You'll want to try everything on one last time once you get the dress home, just to be sure that you have everything. It's a good idea to put everything on—veil, jewelry, dress, all underclothes (except garments if not yet endowed), nylons, and shoes. This would be the time to notice if you see any unseemly lines or the necklace doesn't coordinate, if the shoes are too high or low, or if you forgot nylons.

❑ Have bride pampering time

Find some time for a bubble bath, manicure, pedicure, or nap. Some R & R. It should be close to the wedding, such as the day before or the day of, if there's time. I think it's a fun thing to do with your mom. She'd love the last-minute time with you and it will give her a chance for any last advice. So put in *Steel Magnolias*, grab some Ben and Jerry's, and hang out with Mom.

Tip: Give both yourself and your groom plenty of rest time and date time before the wedding. A date will help you remember why you're doing all this in the first place. It will keep things in perspective and keep you sane. The rest time is so that you don't both spend your honeymoon conked out from exhaustion or worse sick because of it. Rest and relax. It'll be worth it in the end.

chapter thirteen

groom's attire

☐ ## Choose groom's tuxedo

At the actual ceremony, the groom will wear his temple ordinance clothing. The temple will not allow the groom to be married in his tux, even if it's white. Then he will have to change into something for pictures and the reception, as he cannot wear his ordinance clothing outside the temple.

The groom's attire should distinguish him as the groom. Despite popular opinion, the groom gets to pick his own tux. The bride doesn't choose the tux any more than the groom chooses the wedding dress. Ladies, I know you may think that you know what looks good better than your groom does, and you may. However, this is his only wedding too. He should be allowed to express himself as well. It is not, however, inappropriate for you to be invited along to express your loving, supportive, and kind opinion about his options. Remember, you'd expect him to allow you the dress you think looks best without telling you he doesn't like the cut, the color, or the veil. Men care if you like how they look, so let him know what you think is handsome in a positive way rather than telling him that the pastel sixties tux or the jeans and T-shirt are just awful.

Men, you should think through what you'd like a bit before you go to the store as well. Think about cut, color, jacket (do you want tails?), tuxedo shirt or dress shirt (what kind of collar?), cummerbund or vest, and what kind of tie (bow tie, straight tie, or other type).

Now, several people are moving away from the tuxedo and choosing instead to go with a nice suit. My opinion on this is—whatever the groom wants. You're spending a small fortune on the bride wearing a formal gown, so I would say, "groom go formal," but if he hates that and wants to instead spend a couple hundred dollars on a nice suit, that's okay. However, no offense, but I've seen plenty of grooms, hmm . . . change sizes, shall we say, after their wedding. So renting might not be a bad idea.

✎ **Note!** I will from here-on-out refer to the groom's outfit as "tux," whichever way he decides.

❏ Arrange for groom's tuxedo

This step involves ordering the tux that you've chosen. Usually people rent these since purchasing is an expensive and not very common option. Once again, price around and don't be ashamed to use a coupon. They are very popular for tux shops. Find out how long you get the tux for and if you need to clean it before returning it. Also, what else is included in the price? Shoes, vest, tie, cummerbund? Does it need to be altered? Do you need to come back for a second fitting? When can you pick it up? When does it need to be returned? What is the total price? What is the refund and cancellation policy?

❏ Arrange for groom's shoes

The groom's shoes may be included in his tuxedo rental. If not, you'll want to make sure he has shoes to match. It's a good idea to polish up his Sunday shoes, if that's what he's using. Make sure they are comfy; he'll be in them all day and on his feet.

Groom! Your socks should match the color of your pants and shoes. Don't wear your white temple socks with your black tux. Big no no.

❏ Groom's haircut
(Should be done about a week before)

The groom will want to get his hair cut a week or so before the wedding so he doesn't have that "just cut" look. Also, so you can see his face in the pictures.

❑ Pick up groom's tuxedo

Pick up the tux on from the tux shop on the prearranged day. The groom may need to try it on again for the right sizing, so he may need to be the one to go. Make sure you arrange to have it returned for you. Someone else may need to do it if you are going to be on your honeymoon on the date it needs to be returned. So double check the date and time it is to be returned.

❑ Groom's final fitting

You'll want to try everything on one last time once you get to your house. Put everything on. Everything you are going to wear: hat, pants, coat, shirt, tie, cummerbund, vest, cuff links, button studs, socks, underclothes, shoes. Everything. Don't just pick up the tux and check this checkbox. This would be the time to notice if you're missing anything, or if the sleeves are too long, or if the shoes are too tight.

chapter fourteen

family attire &
attendants' dresses

I put the family's and attendants' attire together, because often-times in an LDS wedding, we don't have attendants and, if we do, we tend to use our family.

Family dress is a touchy subject and is very different from wedding to wedding. The decision is different for everyone. Whatever you choose, as with the invitations, keep it consistent and let all involved parties know the plan. First, the mothers of the bride and groom should be in nice (not necessarily matching) dresses. Second, the fathers of the bride and groom should be in either tuxes or very nice suits. Then draw a line and stick to it. Does the whole extended family wear matching dresses and tuxes? Or is simply wearing the wedding color and a nice Sunday outfit enough? I personally prefer the latter. Just make sure that everyone is made aware.

❑ Determine who is wearing tuxedos

The groom's family pays for the groom's tux and the fathers' tuxes only. All other attendants must pay for their own tux. This also includes any matching ties, vests, or cummerbunds. Having said that, determine who in the wedding party will wear tuxes and let them know. Realize that just because you want everyone to wear a tux, doesn't mean they can or will. Outside of the fathers, whose tuxes are paid for by the groom's family, any others may not have the means or the inclination to wear a tux. Be sensitive to what your wedding party wants and can afford when making this decision.

❑ 🕴 Arrange for family tuxedos

Choose and rent the tuxes for the previously determined wedding party members. For ease in understanding, I will from here on out refer to them as family tuxes so as to distinguish them from the groom's tux. Don't forget to shop around! Get details as to what is included, shoes, vest, tie, cleaning fee? Get a total cost and the date of pickup and return. Do they all need to be picked up together? Is a deposit required? How will they fix any last-minute problems? What is their refund and cancellation policy?

Also, try on the tuxes. Many a man has had his mom or wife pick up his tux, only to find out on the wedding day that it doesn't fit and that they paid $80 for the man to look like a boy playing in daddy's closet. Arrange for a fitting and alterations if necessary.

❗ Soapbox Warning

If you are not renting full tuxes but providing ties to multiple members of the wedding party, see if you can get one early, or distribute an actual color match to the wives. I personally have driven myself crazy worrying that "my pain-in-the-neck-to-acquire dress that only slightly matches the wedding color" would clash with my husband's prearranged rented tie, because I didn't get to see its color until the reception. Not to mention trying to coordinate my sons' ties to match my husband's when my husband's tie is MIA. I was patted on the head and told, "Don't worry; it's all taken care of." Yeah, but what color is it? "It's the wedding color." Right, like everything else is exactly the right shade and tone of the wedding color. I know, I'm a freakazoid. Aren't you glad you just get to read my book and move on? My family has to live with me.

❑ Pick up family tuxedos

It is a good idea to have the men pick up their own tuxes, just to verify that the sizing is correct.

❏ Return all rented tuxes

The rental company will have a date and a time for the return. It is wise to return the groom's tux for him at the same time so he doesn't have to worry about it.

❏ Decide mothers' dresses

Each mother pays for her own dress. You'll need to decide if you are going to match or not. You also need to decide if you're going to buy or sew the dresses. You don't have to both buy or both sew. Then, if you're going to match, go shopping ladies. Go shopping together and apart. Look around and decide on something you can both stomach.

❏ Arrange for mothers' dresses

Move ahead to purchasing or sewing your dresses.

❏ Decide on wedding family/attendant attire

This goes back to what I was saying at the beginning of this chapter. Decide who's going to wear what and move forward on it. Everyone is responsible for their own attire. If you want everyone to match exactly, then you are going to have to either arrange a mass shopping trip or buy the fabric for everyone and then disperse it to be made into dresses/ties. Try to choose a style that will flatter different shapes and sizes. Have all your attendants try on the style. If they are out of town, see if they can go to a local sister store to try it on. If you require alterations, the store will likely require a hefty deposit, so be prepared for that. If all the dresses are being sewn for the attendants, be sure to give the seamstress all of the measurement and contact information for everyone so fittings can be easily scheduled. Also, allow for plenty of time.

If you are all going to match, then you may want to think about accessories as well. Can they wear their own or not? Think about, shoes, jewelry, handbags, wraps, whatever matters to you.

One great idea is to have everyone wear black and then provide matching sashes, sweaters, bows, vests, or ties. Or have a different color trim on otherwise identical dresses to give some variety. You could choose a color and fabric and allow the individuals to choose a style that suits them best. There are many options.

If you aren't exactly matching but still want to work together, that is great. The bride's family could all wear one thing, while the groom's family wears another. If the mother of the bride wants to help her whole family with their attire, that is totally normal; however, it is not appropriate for the mother of the bride to tell the groom's family what they must wear after the original decisions have been made.

Let me explain. If it has been decided that everyone will simply wear the wedding color, then everyone gets to decide for themselves. It is inappropriate for the mother of either the bride or the groom at this point to tell everyone, "Oh wait. I think we should all wear skirts, so now you have to." Suggestions and recommendations are welcome; demands start to get touchy. Remember that each person involved in this wedding is his own person, and that most people don't like being told what they and their family are required to purchase and wear, especially if it is something that they really don't like in the first place. Be sensitive. Your family will all be stuck in their outfit for the whole night too, and it'd be great if it was something they could wear again at another occasion. Let them choose something comfortable.

✍ **A Note from the Temple!** It is asked that the family of the bride and groom save the reception attire for the reception. The temple prefers you not wear matching bridesmaids' dresses or mothers' dresses, and certainly not tuxes to the temple. (The groom is the exception.) This includes everyone in matching colors and matching ties, even outside for pictures. Also, the temple facilities should not be clogged up with family members changing into reception attire following a ceremony.

Remember that everyone should be trying to help the couple to dwell on the sacredness and importance of this wedding ceremony. Let the temple be about the ceremony, and save the party attire for the party section of the day. Encourage all those involved to follow the temple guidelines. Let us help keep the sacredness of this wedding for the temple and for the couple.

❑ Decide family's & attendants' shoes

I know this might seem like, "duh," but everyone will want comfortable shoes. They will be stuck on their feet most of the day, and you don't want blisters and sprained ankles. You just don't have time for them, right?

The reason I don't have a checkbox for arranging family attire is that once you have decided on it, it is really their responsibility to arrange for it, not yours. You can't make them do what you want, (only beg, bribe, charm, coerce, and cry), so it is now in their hands to make sure they have an outfit for the reception.

❑ EVERYONE try on their wedding attire

I'm not sure how to emphasize this strongly enough. Everyone. All of you, Moms, Dads, siblings, attendants, babies, everyone. Did I say everyone?

Try it on. At home. With your chosen wedding underwear and socks. Make sure everyone has their slips, jewelry, bras, nylons, hairpieces, ties, cummerbunds, black socks, button studs, cuff links, shirts, pants, coats, and hats. Everything. Try the whole ensemble on. It will really help make sure you have everything you need.

Then, put it all away together so later you don't have to rummage around trying madly as you run out the door to find that last earring or cuff link, screaming the whole way and ruining the entire day. No, I'm totally kidding. It will way not ruin the day. It's just clothes. Calm down. But it really is a good idea to keep it together for ease on the wedding day.

chapter fifteen

reception

❑ Determine type of reception

You need to know what kind of reception you are going for. The options are limitless:
- Small and intimate dinner
- Casual open house
- Semi-formal with many guests coming through a line.
- BBQ
- Dancing and Toasts

The list really goes on and on. It's up to you and your style. However . . .

Before deciding on your reception style and plan, ask yourself who you're planning it for. The last thing you want is angry and annoyed guests. When planning any other sort of gathering with people, you always plan around what your guests would like to eat, do, and see. Why should a wedding reception be any different? The point of a wedding reception is for well-wishers to come and celebrate not only your marriage but also marriage as an institution. It is a time for them to give you their congratulations and to show their support of your particular marriage. And of course, to give you gifts. Why would you want to annoy or upset them? One big point of this reception should be to give them an appropriate place and time to express these things. Their comfort is not more important than your own, but it should be kept in mind throughout the planning process.

! Soapbox Warning

We don't often think about what a touching and sweet thing it is that this network of friends is getting together to help you create a household that can sustain a family. We think, "Oh, I'm going to have to shake hands with tons of people" and "Oh, I'm going to have to stand for hours"; but every person that comes to your reception is saying, "I believe in families. I support this family you are just beginning. Here's a present. Have a good family." That's what every one of them is doing when they bring you a gift. They say to themselves, "Remember when we got married and we didn't have this?" or "Remember when we got married and someone gave us one of these and it made such a difference?" It's not just, "Oh gosh, someone got married. Quick let's stop at the 7-Eleven and buy them a soda pop." These guests of yours are taking their time and their money to support your potential family. There's a great significance that goes overlooked in all the hubbub of just getting things arranged for the wedding. There's a huge tradition of family building that's being expressed in this reception that you might miss if you don't pay attention to it. Instead you might just see a big party.

❑ Decide on a color

This is just to help everyone have a jumping-off point. What colors do you want? Consider your favorites as well as what colors suit you. Season may also be a factor. Using complementary colors can help spruce it up and avoid sensory overload. You could also use different shades of the same color. This does make it easier for someone to find a match, because there's more choices.

Remember, though that you need to be specific in your color. My dad always says there are "boy colors" and "girl colors." It all has to do with how specific your color is. He says, "All the colors in an 8-count crayon box are 'boy colors' and all the others are 'girl colors.'" So you can't just say "red," because maybe you mean Christmas red or burgundy or fuchsia. Give everyone who is planning wedding items a clear-cut idea of a specific color. A good way to do this is to use fabric swatches or paint samples. Then everyone is on the same page.

If you're going to have a theme, such as the navy or Halloween or cowboy, this is the place to decide that as well. A theme is neither necessary nor expected, but it is an option.

❏ Map out the reception layout

This layout will give you a general idea. You will make more specific and firm plans in the decorating phase. Begin to decide where the guests will enter and exit. Where will the receiving line be? The cake? The gift table? The guest tables? Where will the bride and groom be at the different intervals? These and all other layout questions need to be answered. Basically, figure out where each aspect of your reception will be physically. The bride and groom should always be visible to the majority of the room. (Even while they are seated. Try a platform for their table if necessary.)

❏ Determine reception program

If you are going to have a program at your reception, this is the time to outline it. If not, this would be a good time to finalize your reception timeline (cake cutting, bouquet throwing, dancing, departure). Should you decide to have a program, it's best to put it about halfway through the evening so the largest number of guests will catch it.

Programs at receptions are not required, although, depending on the area in which you live, they are sometimes expected. They, like all aspects of your celebration, can be as grand or simple as you like. You could have toasts, speeches, or songs sung to or by the bridal couple. Whatever works for you. If you are having dancing, this is also a good time to lay out the order of the dances and who will be involved in which ones (couple's first dance, bride and father, groom and mother, and so forth). Just find a place in the reception timeline and place it there. You can do toasts and speeches during the dinner to cut back on the program length. Make sure everyone involved is aware of their involvement so they can prepare, and don't forget to give a written program to your band/DJ/MC.

❑ Print a written program, if desired

This is only done if you are having a program at all. It can be accomplished many ways. You could print one large program and have it displayed at the reception, perhaps by the entrance. You could print several handheld programs and have them available at the entrance to the reception or waiting at the tables for the guests as they are seated. You can even have just one program per table and place it out with the centerpieces.

❑ Ask people to help at the reception; assign specific jobs

If you're not using a professional reception hall, you will have lots of things at the actual reception that will need to be seen to and babysat: setup, take down, escorting of older guests through the line, hosting of the reception, sitting at the guest book or handling the gifts. This is on top of all the other assignments, such as: picking up the cake or tuxes or any rental items, cooking, sewing, serving—the responsibility list goes on.

It is a good idea to make yourself the director and not the person in charge of all grunt work. This will help you to be able to sit back and enjoy the actual wedding day instead of running around crazily trying to do everything yourself.

You may choose to use family, friends, ward members, or to hire people. No matter what you decide, you need to ask the people if they are willing. For some people, it will be an honor to be asked, but don't just sign people up thinking, "They won't mind." You can never know what someone has on their plate until you try to add to it.

❗ Soapbox Warning

Be decisive and don't waste people's time. There is room for shopping around, but there is also a time for deciding. For instance: Shop around for a caterer, but once you've chosen one and you go to the caterer to order the food for the reception, don't spend time tasting and choosing and then say, "Okay, we have to go check with the groom's mom, so we'll let you know." You've just wasted the caterer's time. Take all the people with you who have a deciding vote. Make a decision and move on. This holds true for several aspects of the reception, including: photography, decorating, cake designs, floral arrangements, and so on.

When you ask for help for the wedding, you need to also have a specific job for them. Otherwise people all start trying to do the same job and something gets overlooked. If you've made everyone's responsibility clear, there'll be a lot less trouble, fewer arguments, and a lot more efficiency.

Also, when people offer to help, say, "Thanks. I'll let you know." Don't just agree blindly. You don't know if you will need or want their help until you have a specific view of what help is needed. This approach will help you avoid hurting feelings by having to go back to them later and telling them, "No, I really don't need you to do that."

Lastly, once you have decided and assigned all of your people to help, you will need to review and remind them all throughout the whole process. Just make sure they are still on task or that they are still planning on helping on the day of or whatever their responsibility is.

❑ Determine wedding receiving line

I've seen weddings that have no receiving line, just the couple walking around chatting. The direct opposite to this is also done in a large receiving line complete with couple, parents, in-laws, siblings, groomsmen, and bridesmaids. I have problems with both these extremes.

My favorite wedding line is: bride's dad, bride's mom, bride, groom, groom's mom, groom's dad—in that order. The reason is that no person that comes to your reception will be someone who at least one of those six people doesn't know. It gives your guests an opportunity to congratulate the couple and the parent that they know. The reason for my order of the line is the moms always want to stand next to their sweet babies, right? And the bride's parents should go first, seeing as it's their little girl and they generally constitute the title of host and hostess of the reception. (Exception—if either parents are divorced, then you determine who all you want in the line. If they get along well, they may not mind standing near one another. However, you may have to switch up the order to make it more comfortable for your parents to both be in the line. You could separate the bride's parents by using the groom's parents or the bridal couple as interference.)

You don't have to have a receiving line for the entirety of your reception. If you want a chance to mingle, eat, dance at your reception, you can indicate so on the invitation by stating, "Receiving line from 6:00–7:30 p.m., Dancing from 7:30–8:30 p.m." Or some-such. A great way to handle the ending of a formal receiving line is to send a bridesmaid or groomsman to the end of the line of guests entering and let newcomers know that the receiving line is closing and that they can just go right into the reception. Make sure he stops the line with time to spare though, so you can finish greeting the guests already waiting in line and still maintain your time line.

! Soapbox Warning

Now, here are the reasons I don't think the other two choices I mentioned are the best. When there is no official line and the couple is walking through the crowd, it doesn't give all the guests an opportunity to congratulate the couple. It is very important to give your guests this opportunity. You may think that you are more approachable walking around than in a line. That's ridiculous! Normal, polite people, who are your parents' friends, won't interrupt a conversation you are having just to say, "Hello, I'm an obscure person to you, but I had to buy you a gift and drive all the way down here because I love your mom and dad." So find a place to stand still to greet your guests who have taken time out of their own busy lives to celebrate this amazing time of your life.

The second scenario that I don't like is the ginormous line with everyone in it. Most guests don't really care who your best friend is or your little sister. And it's not very nice of you to make your best friend and your little sister stand in a giant line all night and shake hands with people who don't even care about them. The best way to honor your friends and siblings is to ask them to remain through the reception to share in the joy, to get to talk with the people they do know and that do care about them, and to get to sit and eat goodies the whole time. Doesn't that sound great? Even Joyful? Plus, then your guests will get through the line faster and continue on to enjoying themselves, and that's the point of the whole thing, right? Joy.

Keeping the receiving line short and moving will really help keep your guests happy. A larger receiving line slows down the guests and increases the wait time. Keep the guests moving. You may think, "Oh I barely talked to them for a few minutes," but if each person in the line talks to each guest for "a few minutes," it really adds up and suddenly you have a long line of guests waiting hours just to say congratulations. Think about it. I don't even like to wait an hour to ride Space Mountain. That's why Disneyland gives out those fast pass tickets. We live in a world of instant gratification. We are not used to waiting.

❑ Ask members of line to join

If you are going to have attendants, this is the checkbox for inviting them to be such. Don't just assume the members of the wedding line know that they are to be in it. Ask them, invite them, and thank them for being willing.

❑ Select room for bride and groom to change clothing

You will want a room, like the junior chapel or priesthood rooms in a church house, to change your clothes. You need somewhere that is a bit off the beaten track so guests won't be passing your stuff as they come and go to the reception. Don't use the bathroom to change in. It's not clean or roomy for putting on your dress, and it will be needed by your guests. You may also want to bring a mirror for the selected changing room. Make sure you have privacy, though. Lock the room behind you or post a sign or a guard at the door. Just something that stops people from accidentally walking in on you changing.

I personally think it's a good idea to change out of your wedding attire before leaving the reception. The groom will generally have to anyway so that his tux can be returned while you are on the honeymoon. The wedding dress may or may not have to be returned, but it's a good idea to leave it and not pack it around on the honeymoon. This will keep it from getting dirty or damaged.

❑ Make a plan for children at reception

It is a good idea to consider a few things for children to do who are stuck hanging around the reception all night. Ideas might include: kid-friendly food (such as hot dogs or mac 'n cheese) if your chosen food isn't kid friendly, coloring pages and crayons, some sort of craft, or even a movie in another room. If you are serving a full meal and having dancing at the reception, that should be enough to entertain the children. But if it's a lot of sitting around and talking, the kids may get bored; and after tugging on your arm and screaming for an hour or so, they may get rowdy.

❑ ❦ Arrange for bride/groom departure

You need to decide beforehand how the reception is going to end. Will you wait for all the guests to leave, or will the bride and groom just leave at the end time, and everyone else cleans up, and the late guests don't see them? Have a plan because it won't be natural, and you'll be tired and want to have someone just say, "Okay, it's over now. You can leave."

Decide if you are going to change your clothes or make your exit in full dress. Make sure your car is ready with gas and waiting (have a trusted person bring it around for you). If you haven't eaten, ask someone to bring out some food for you to take with you as well.

! Soapbox Warning

Throwing rice, flowers, or confetti, or having your guests blow bubbles or light sparklers as you exit the reception, can be done but is not required. Be careful. It can be annoying to some guests, so don't force anyone to participate. There are laws against throwing certain things, and cleanup is instantly required no matter what is used. Also keep in mind that some things may stain your clothes or become slippery. Other things catch on fire or get in your eyes. Think it through and determine if it's worth it to you.

And here comes another:

! Soapbox Warning

No one in the wedding planning circle should instigate decorating the bridal couple's car. If the bride just has to have it decorated, her mom may want to tell others to do it, to make the bride happy. Don't! Is she not happy enough? Isn't having all this other stuff revolving around making her happy? I have been told before that I needed to decorate the car (which I personally think is tacky, but etiquette-wise it's socially totally acceptable) for a bride to be happy, when I was barely tolerating the bride as it was, and I was a remote family member on the groom's side and didn't particularly like her. Things like decorating the car are optional things that if her friends or siblings want to do, they can and will. Mom, don't tell them to. It's supposed to be for fun, and it's supposed to be a surprise.

Whoa! Now I got that out of my system.

If you must decorate the car, be careful that any items used do not damage the car. And please be kind. I know one couple whose family rewired the car to honk every time the brake was pressed. It was humiliating for the couple, especially with the addition of a "honk if you're . . ." sign. You get the picture. It made the bride cry, and they went to the nearest house to call for help. Make sure that both the bride and the groom think it's okay to have their car decorated. Bride and groom, if it isn't okay with you, then make that well known to everyone you can.

Having said all that, the groom will want to arrange for how the couple is going to leave. Some like to use their own car, but some like to go with a limo or a horse and carriage. Just make sure it's been thought of and decided.

Favors

I don't think favors are common enough to be expected. They are fine if you're willing to do one more thing. But they are an extra thing. Don't drive yourself crazy trying to do them. You don't have to, and you can save money by leaving this out.

If you'd like to do this, some couples have a label made to put on a candy bar, bottle, or package of candy. Other couples have their names printed on napkins. Some put out jars of candy and bags, so guests can fill their own favor bag. You could have a special thought from the couple such as a scripture or poem printed on nice paper and tied with a ribbon. You could also distribute small candles or flowers. These are fine ideas if you really want to, just don't make the "favor" double as the "thank you note." Some believe if they put a big "Thanks!" with the couple's names on it, then that is a sufficient thank you for their guests. It's not. If you're having a favor, have a favor, and then also write thank you notes to everyone. Cool? Cool.

chapter sixteen

food

Food is a big one. This can be a big expense and a lot of work. Or it can be much cheaper and even more work. Or it can be expensive and little to no work. Or it can be simple and cheap. It's all a matter of budget and preference.

❏ Choose and hire a caterer or choose and arrange for food help

Here is where a lot of people jump the gun. They think, "I can't possibly do it myself. It's too daunting." So they hire an expensive caterer. Or they think, "No matter what we're doing, we can do it cheaper and easier ourselves. Who wants to waste money on a caterer?"

Slow down and think things through. This decision needs to combine with the next step of deciding a menu. Think about how complicated your treat, snack, or meal will be. Think about prep work, setup, maintenance throughout the reception, and cleanup. Think about, what you will do if the food runs out. Caterers will take care of all of this for you. They use formulas to determine expected guest counts from number of invitations issued. They will not bother you throughout the reception, leaving you to concentrate on your guests and your sweet day. I think having a caterer helps keep the whole reception lower stress and increases the overall joy.

Having said that, you want to shop around. Each caterer offers very different things. Some have specific menus to choose from while others are more open to create what you want. Some include the dishes to eat off and some don't. Some include servers and linens. Ask what their specific services include and arrange for a tasting so you'll have a sample of what they can actually do and not just what they say they can do. Make sure you get their estimate in writing, including what deposits are expected and what the cancellation and refund policies are.

Or you could find a friend or someone who used to be a caterer or wedding planner and now just does it for fun or on the side. These people exist, and they are super cheap and very qualified. Ask around. If you do have to hire a professional caterer, get a few bids. Don't go with the first one you find just because they assure you a low price. Make them prove it. Take a few competitor bids back to them and see if they lower theirs.

Remember, almost all reception halls will require you to use their catering.

You can also do something in the middle. See if the caterer will serve food you planned and/or prepared. There might be a compromise available.

Now, if you decide to do it yourself, you'll want to plan ahead for bumps in the road. First, think through how difficult your menu is. How will you keep food warm or cold? You'll need help in the kitchen, but not so many people that they get in each other's way. You need to clearly define one person as the person in charge. Everyone needs to be made aware that that certain person is in charge. Oh, and the person in charge, should absolutely not be one of the wedding party. No matter what. They will have other things to attend to.

You will probably have to revisit this checkbox after you have determined your menu. That will give you a better idea of what kind of help you are even going to need.

You are also going to want at least a vague estimate of number of people you are expecting. This number will change as you complete your guest lists and as people start to talk with you more about the upcoming day.

❏ Select menu for reception

When deciding your menu for the reception keep in mind: cost, preparation, does it need to be kept cold or warm, how will you distribute it to your guests, how messy is it, how generally well liked is it, how annoying is the clean-up? Do you want to serve cake if you will also being serving your wedding cake at the end of the reception? Do you want a big, hot, heavy meal in August? Or should you lean more toward salads and a lighter overall menu? Don't worry too much about the calorie count. It's your wedding day. Have something you truly enjoy.

Don't forget beverages when deciding. Punch? Soft drinks? Lemon water? Determine how they will be distributed as well.

The two biggest issues here are preparation and distribution.

❏ Determine how food will be prepared

This will not be your problem at all if using a caterer. However, should you have to handle preparation yourselves . . .

Pre-made can be a good idea. Also, just because you aren't using a caterer doesn't mean you can't use a bakery or deli. If you have your local bakery prepare éclairs, brownies, sheet cake, or whatnot, then all your kitchen help has to do is serve up the plates and distribute them. Same goes with a chicken salad, BBQ ribs, or a simple cheese or veggie tray at the deli, making the whole affair quite simple. Or you could purchase some of the refreshments at Costco or some other big-box store. Simply lay them out beautifully on a nice serving tray and "Voila!" You could throw in some mints, nuts, or a scoop of ice cream to add a bit more, if you like.

If you make the goodies yourself, try to choose things that can be prepared in bulk beforehand and then served at the reception. It is difficult to keep food at anything but room temperature. If you are a novice, I would recommend items that can be set out and remain out. Although, if you have to choose, it's easier to keep things cold if they come straight out of the kitchen and into the guest's hands.

❑ Determine how food will be distributed

The choices that are most popular are buffet, prepared plates set out on a table, or people serving guests after they are seated.

Buffet or several food stations

This is nationally the most popular choice among LDS couples. The good thing about this method is that the guests serve themselves. You will need people to refill and monitor the food on the buffet table, but it takes a lot fewer people than having it served to the guests as they arrive and sit down. If you are not using a caterer, a buffet is overall easier to manage then any of the other options. It is also beneficial to break up your buffet table into smaller, more specific food stations. Such as: desserts, candies, meat carving, and beverage. This will break up the giant line and allow guests to more quickly move to their desired food.

The problems are numerous. It is more difficult to keep things warm or cold—especially really cold, like ice cream. Because the guests serve themselves, they take as much as they want, making it harder to judge how much food you need. A buffet tends to be messier and can be harder to maintain. Food may get mixed in the pots as well as dropped on the table and floor while being served. Lastly, some people don't like the idea of buffets because strangers, who may not have the same cleanliness level you deem necessary, are handling what is potentially their food.

Prepared plates on a serving table

This method still gives you the advantage of guests serving themselves but eliminates several of the downsides to a buffet. You still need people to make the plates up in the kitchen and bring them out to the serving table. The downside that remains is that while it does cut down on people taking more than they need, it doesn't completely stop it. People, especially children, will come back for another plate or two, or even sneak things off plates sitting on the serving table while their parents aren't looking.

Serving guests after they are seated

If doing a full meal instead of just appetizers or desserts, people often think that a seated meal is more expensive. That can be true, but shop around. Sometimes the benefit of an exact guest count can outweigh the need for a caterer to provide extra food for any people making return trips to a buffet. The benefits to this method are: cleanliness, portion control, and easier maintenance of food temperature. You'll need people to load the plates in the kitchen and people to serve the plates to the guests. The biggest problems are that you have to manage serving people; and since guests don't decide everything they have on their plate, they don't always eat everything you give them.

✍ **Note!** If having a formal, sit-down meal, other things will need to be decided. I won't go into detail, as these are not common among a traditional, middle class, LDS wedding. But should you wish to do one, here are some general items to discuss.

- will you have people RSVP an entrée choice?
- how will you handle seating? (If guests are being served different choices, assigned seating will be better for the serving staff.)
- if you have assigned seating, you'll need table numbers that are easy to identify and place cards (these can be done many creative ways—use your imagination)

No matter what you choose, there are people who are going to love it and people who are not going to like it at all. Remember that you are the one who has to pay for it and deal with the consequences. You need to weigh the options. Think it through thoroughly and decide.

One last thing to consider: allergies. You can't possibly make an allergy-free menu for all your guests, but you will want to consider common allergies. Most people who have strong allergies will just stay clear of things for themselves. But if, for example the use of peanuts isn't clear, you may want to make it clear.

❑ Decide what reception "paper or china" goods are needed

You'll need to decide what dishes are needed for your refreshments—cups, plates, bowls, cutlery, and napkins. You'll also need to decide how you want them to look: clear, plastic, glass, china, napkins that are your chosen color, and so on. Just decide so they can be priced and purchased. Remember, renting is always an option as well. Check with the reception center and caterer. Dishes may or may not be included. The ward dishes are always an option as well, although not the fanciest option.

Want something a bit more elegant? Consider combining several Thanksgiving or china sets from family and close friends. It can be quaint to have mismatched settings. You could do a whole table the same or even mix up a bowl from one set and plate from another.

❑ Purchase reception plates, cups, utensils

Purchase the dishes needed for refreshments. If you are renting or borrowing, this is the check box for that as well. If you are buying, think about quality. Sometimes it's worth it to pay more for a better quality. Places like party stores tend to be a lot cheaper, but their cups will crumble in your hands, their forks break in your food, and their plates can't withstand the weight. You don't want to have to buy twice as many as you need because they keep breaking. You should, however, buy more than you need just in case. In case of what? In case a lightning bolt hits the church targeting only the plates. In case of everything.

❑ Order or buy reception food

Purchase the predetermined food. Don't forget to shop around and ask questions. Some places will discount if you're buying in bulk.

❑ Prepare reception food

If you are the one preparing it, do so. If not, double check that it is being prepared.

❏ Arrange for cleanup of food and all food areas

Generally this is as simple as asking the people who are helping in the kitchen to clean it all up and move out of there. They are usually expecting such a thing and are happy to do so.

You will also want to think about garbage placement at the reception. You should have a garbage, either in the room, or right outside the door. Remember, guests will generate garbage from things they bring in themselves, as well as from anything you give them. So if you have people bussing the tables of the refreshment garbage, keep in mind that there will also be: tissues, gum wrappers, diapers, and so on. People will need a place to put those things, other than leaving them on the tables to be cleared away.

You will need a plan for anything that is being kept. Where does it need to go? Who will take it there? If there are any rentals, their return will also need to be arranged. Make sure someone besides you knows what needs to be done with everything.

❏ Determine what is to be done with leftovers

If you have planned well, there will undoubtedly be leftovers. A caterer will take care of that herself. However, any other kitchen help will need to be instructed as to what to do with the leftovers—how to package them and where to take them.

Tip: It's a nice idea to pack a bag of leftovers for the bridal couple to take with them that night. Odds are, they haven't eaten as much as they've visited.

❏ Provide means to deal with leftovers

Provide containers, baggies, or any such thing to get the leftovers to their destination.

chapter seventeen

cake

This cake is the wedding cake. *The* wedding cake. There may be other cakes associated with your wedding or reception, but this chapter is for handling the details of the one—the only—*the* wedding cake.

❏ Decide if you will be serving the cake at the reception

You need to know if your wedding cake will be served or just displayed at the wedding reception. This decision will impact all further cake decisions within this chapter. It will help you determine if you care about things like: taste, size, and ability to be disassembled.

❏ Decide on a cake decorator

This is one of those things that if you decide to have a friend do it for you, you have to be totally all right with it being awful. If you are using a novice, choose a simple design, preferably something you've seen your decorator accomplish successfully before. You could even have a bakery make a simple white cake and have your friend add embellishments, such as flowers or ribbons.

When choosing a cake decorator, look at cost and shop around. Look at bakeries, caterers, grocery stores, wholesale stores (like Costco), and individuals. Ask about taste tests. Will they allow you to try their cake? Is there an added charge for tasting? This will be especially important as you narrow down flavors of cake and frosting. You'll want to get a sense of their work. Ask about delivery and setup charges, and get all estimates in writing. Think about how much the cake is worth to you, and remember they are difficult to make and time consuming, but it is just a cake.

❑ Decide on a cake design

Think about what you want done with the cake. Is it going to be merely displayed, or will it be served? If it's going to be displayed only, you could use styrofoam molds. The frosting can be different as well, because it doesn't have to be eaten. You can also use fabric, ribbon, or flowers to decorate instead of frosting.

If you are going to serve the cake, you'll need to think about how it will be cut and served, what it will look like as it's cut, and how it will taste. It will have to be disassembled, so it will need to be constructed with this idea in mind.

When I say think about how the cake will look as it's cut, I mean that a wedding cake on display should always look as appetizing as possible. If you have to completely tear it apart to serve it, no one will want a piece. Think about using more icing and less ribbon or flowers so that as it's cut, it looks very much the same as it did on display.

You will want it to taste good, for both yourself and your guests. You can choose from many different kinds of cake. There are options as far as frosting and filling, as well. Examples: vanilla cake with citrus filling and buttercream frosting or a chocolate cake with a whipped pudding filling and a caramel frosting. It doesn't even have to be a cake at all. You can go crazy and use pies, cupcakes, or a dessert bar. One friend of mine with several allergies stepped outside of tradition and had a cake ice sculpture. It's all about what suits you and your groom.

The kinds of cake will impact the decoration. For instance, some cakes, like chocolate and spice, are heavier and so need to be used as the bottom layer only or be well supported on higher levels. Some frostings don't hold up in the heat and humidity. You may have to be flexible on the cake design if you aren't flexible on the cake and frosting flavors. A professional decorator will have insight into this. If using a novice, you might want to search for lighter cakes. You'd hate to have your guests skin their knees rushing to save the falling cake thirty minutes into your reception. True story.

Have at least a vague idea of what you'd like before you go cake shopping. Do you want multiple layers? Round, square, or hexagon? Do you want three or four smaller cakes displayed on pedestals? How big do you want it? Have at least a few ideas in mind to help narrow down your options and, as always, keep your budget in mind.

Many weddings have a groom's cake as well, although this is not at all required or expected. The groom's cake is usually smaller and displayed somewhere near the wedding cake at the reception. He generally chooses this cake, and it is less formal, speaking more to his personal interests.

❑ Choose a cake topper

Wedding cakes do not require a topper, but they are more common than not. You can use many different things: flowers (whether fresh or candy), a temple, a couple, bows, and so on. Whatever works for you. Just choose what you would like.

❑ Acquire cake topper

Purchase or order the topper you decided upon in the previous step.

❑ Order cake

Communicate your desired cake design to the cake decorator and then say "go forth and create!"

❑ Arrange for cake to get to reception

You'll need to make arrangements to get the cake to the reception. Some cake decorators will deliver for you, but you may have to get someone else to pick it up.

❑ Purchase cake-cutting utensils

Generally, special cake-cutting and serving utensils are purchased for the bride and groom to cut the cake and serve it to each other. These can be purchased at bakeries, kitchen stores, party stores, or just your friendly neighborhood grocery store. They are labeled as wedding-cake-cutting utensils and are usually found with the party supplies. The utensils are generally displayed on the table next to the cake throughout the reception so as to be at hand when the bride and groom are ready for the cake cutting.

❑ Determine how cake will be displayed

This can be as simple as a small round table covered in a tablecloth or as big as a gazebo and surrounding mirrors. You could set a few flowers on the table or a picture of the couple. It's up to you. This can be discussed with your room decorator. She will have ideas for how to set it up, and then she can handle setting the stage for the cake to arrive and be placed.

If your cake is something other than a traditional wedding cake, you will need to make it clear that it is in fact "the" cake. For example: if your cake is made of cupcakes, candy, Twinkies, or ice cream cones, you'll want to put up a sign or have a person attend the cake.

This is to avoid people mistaking the cake for refreshments and eating it. If a guest starts to prematurely eat the cake and you have to stop them, this will be embarrassing for both parties involved. Better to preemptively avoid it.

❑ Determine when cake will be cut

You'll want to decide when to have the bride and groom cut the cake. Have someone be in charge of breaking into the line and assuring it happens. You'll want to do this a bit early (say, the last half hour of the reception) if you are serving the cake. The line can resume after the cutting. It is customary, when serving the cake to one another, that the groom feed the bride first.

This is also a good time to throw the bouquet and garter. The reason you'll want a determined time is that it's possible that your line of guests will not have a break, and you'll never get out of there.

! Soapbox Warning

Feeding the wedding cake to each other is a sweet tradition, the origins of which are disputed. Most people agree it came from

Roman times, when they would crinkle wheat over the bride's head to symbolize fertility. Nowadays it's believed to symbolize your sharing of a household, how you'll care for one another, and your commitment to provide for one another. Take your pick. Do not shove the cake into each other's faces. That's so inappropriate. It's rude to each other, it's rude to your guests, and it spits in the face of what the tradition is there for in the first place. It is so not funny and totally not wedding etiquette. Don't do it! Be sweet, be loving, be kind.

❑ Determine how cake will be served and by whom

Choose a person (or two—not too many) to cut and serve up the plates of cake. Generally the cake is simply set out, as guests are right there just waiting for a piece.

Think about how you want it cut and how big you want the pieces to be. Be careful. Discuss cutting ideas with the cake decorator. She will have suggestions to make sure the cake doesn't topple.

❑ Purchase cake serving goods

Purchase small plates, forks, and napkins if you are going to serve the cake to your guests. Refer to the section on purchasing reception plates in chapter sixteen.

❑ Make arrangements for uneaten cake

Someone will need to get rid of the cake. Whether letting the children at it or having it bronzed, it needs a plan and someone to execute it. (The plan, that is.)

chapter eighteen

decorations

When deciding what decorations you want, you need to see them, not just hear about them. Look at pictures at least for a tentative decision, and if possible the real thing, before the reception. That way you'll really know what you're getting into.

❑ Decide reception decorations and layout

Layout

When deciding your decorations, you really need to have your reception venue in mind the whole time. Is there room for that gazebo? Can you really fit nine tables? How are you going to get that large set piece in the door? How are you going to cart all the decoration items to your location? Is there room for a dance floor?

If you're having a sit-down meal, even if you aren't having assigned seating, you'll need to know where the bridal couple will be seated. Do you want your own table? Or a head table for you and your parents? It is best to make sure the bridal couple can be seen by all or at least the majority of the room so your guests can ogle you. Once you decide, make sure to have your seats marked as reserved so others won't take them.

Tip: It's better to use fewer chairs at each table. Set eight chairs there instead of ten in order to give your guests plenty of room to breathe and to make them not feel packed in.

As you think about this and explore your options, it is a good idea to create a layout map for your decorators. That way you all have the same vision, and since someone else will be setting up for you, likely without you there, it'll be what you hoped to see upon your arrival. Keep in mind the flow of your guests in your layout as well.

You will also want to have a place for people to sit. This is for people who will be hanging around the reception for a long period of time but aren't standing in line, sitting at the book, guarding the cake, arranging the presents, or eating. Are there enough tables for everyone to remain at their table, or do they need to rotate out? People will want to linger. You need to leave that as an option. A good solution for this is to simply line a couple of walls with chairs. You could also have several small groupings of chairs placed around the room for such a thing.

If you are going to have dancing, you need to leave an open area for the dance floor—whether you're bringing a floor in or just clearing a space.

You need to decide where you are getting everything. Tables, chairs, backdrops, a tent, pillars—anything you are using. You need to know where it's all coming from, who's setting it up, and where and how it's going to get put back.

Decoration Options

If you are using a professional decorator, she'll have ideas and pictures and charts. If you are thinking up the decorations yourself, look around for ideas—look everywhere. Check out hotels you go to, magazines you read (and not just bridal magazines), and stores you visit. Pay attention to your favorite places. What draws you to them? See if you can imitate it. Look on the Internet. The possibilities are endless. You'd be surprised what will inspire you. Walk through craft stores, Walmart, Oriental Trading, Home Depot, and IKEA. Check out friends' houses and your own home. There are many books and websites available with ideas for sprucing up cultural halls and backyards.

Look around for those random bits of lace and flowers you have tucked into boxes. For example: you can tie a piece of lace around the back of a chair to make it look more elegant, even add a place-card tucked in. You'd be amazed at how beautiful a thing you can create with nothing but leftover craft supplies and your imagination. Use: beads, marbles, old dried flowers, pots, jars, and vases. Be open to ideas, especially your own.

❑ Check over lighting

Lighting needs to be taken into consideration as well. This may be as simple as flipping on the light switch. But it too can be as involved as you make it. Would you like to have lighting be a part of the centerpieces and then only turn on part of the lights? Would you like twinkling lights hung as decorations? Remember, if you are using lamps, twinkling lights, candles, or the headlights off a 747 as part of your decorations, your overall lighting will be affected. Be careful though. There are no lit candles allowed in any ward house. You'll need to make other arrangements if that's desired.

If you are outside, you may need to think about how you'll keep it light once the sun goes down. Also consider if you need electricity for your band or DJ. If you are using any sort of reception center, they will have lighting pretty well sorted out.

❑ Determine flow of guests

Determining where your guests are going to park, which door they'll come in, how they'll drop off their gift, how they'll greet the line, how they'll view the cake, where they'll sit to eat, and how they'll exit are all within this category.

You need to make all of these aspects very clear. I know it sounds terrible, but herd your guests like cattle. Leave them no other option than the way you want them to go. It is especially important that you make it very clear where they park and where they are to enter the reception. Using the decorations is a good method.

You will also want to think about the older people waiting in line to speak to the bridal couple. This line tends to be long and slow moving. You may want to set up chairs along the line's route so older people, sick people, or pregnant women may sit as they wait to speak to you. You could even have someone assigned to watch for older or frail people and to escort them straight to the front of the line.

❑ Arrange for reception decorations

Once you've decided what you'd like and where you'd like it to go, you need to procure it. Make it appear. Rent it, borrow it, build it. Whatever method you're using, arrange for it to be done.

❑ Arrange for reception venue to be decorated

Now, some people decide they can do this themselves. My recommendation is, if you're going to decorate the church yourself, then do it the night before, not the day of the wedding. When I say "yourself," I mean anyone in the wedding party.

The entire wedding party is going to be too busy on the day of the wedding to go to the venue and set up. Let this not be a stressful day full of rushing to and fro trying to do it all yourself. Let others do it for you. It will give you the time to just be happy and reflect on this exciting day. You will have much less anxiety, and it will really help contribute to the overall joyfulness of the day.

Whomever you decide to have set up needs to be specifically asked, have everything explained to them, and then be confirmed as the big day approaches. They will also need a key or a contact who can let them into the venue.

❑ Arrange for decoration cleanup

This can easily just be the same people who set up for you. The wedding party may decide at this point to help, but remember, you will be tired. It will have been a long day. The bridal couple should leave and not help cleanup. Also, everyone will need specific instructions as to where everything goes once it's cleaned up, both things staying within the building and things that are taken away.

chapter nineteen

centerpieces

Often centerpieces get grouped in with either your decorations or your flowers, although they don't have to be grouped and are a small way that you can express yourself separate from the decorations.

❑ Decide linens

You'll need something to cover the tables where your guests will be seated, but you should also think about the other tables, such as the gift, food, and cake tables, and any other linens that may be necessary. I'll talk more about the other tables in their specific categories. For the tables where your guests are seated, think about what food you are serving. Do you want plain white cloth tablecloths when you're serving red punch that is likely to spill and stain? Do you want something that will wipe off easier? Or if white is your desire, can you provide extras as replacements, in case a spill occurs? Just keep the food that will be served in mind.

In choosing linens, you can use accent colors. For instance: save money by using the ward's Relief Society tablecloths, then add a splash of color with a square of fabric cut out in your colors. You could also have the same effect using lace or tulle. Be creative.

❑ Decide centerpieces

You need to again remember your guests when deciding on centerpieces. Be careful of any that take up so much table space that the guests have little room. You also want your guests to be able to talk and celebrate with each other, so make sure your centerpieces are short enough to see over or tall enough to comfortably see under. Remember, no lit candles inside the church. But there are still dozens, dare I say hundreds, of ideas: flameless candles, marbles in jars, fruit, candy, flowers, pictures of the couple, disposable cameras, cakes, stacks of books, mirrors, lamps, a drink dispenser, or a pitcher.

Jars are a wonderful way to go. Ask around for jars, pitchers, vases, glasses, even baskets or boxes. Then fill them up with flower petals, colored water, candy, sand, rocks, or bunched fabric. You could surround the centerpieces with confetti, ribbons, petals, or pretty rocks to add an extra effect.

You can even have edible centerpieces, especially if you have a children's table. Make it from a stack of cupcakes, candies, or strawberries. Use your imagination.

This is another place that it is a good idea to look around people's houses. You can get a lot of different ideas from surprising places.

The centerpieces don't have to all be the same—be daring and mix it up. Have some be very elaborate while keeping others simple.

❏ Create, buy, or borrow centerpieces

Whatever your deal is, make it happen. If you are adding it to the florist or decorator, this is that step.

❏ Arrange for centerpieces/table setup

Usually the decorator sets up the tables. You can arrange with her to set up just the tables and chairs or to add the tablecloths, or to do the whole shebang including the centerpieces.

If you are renting, you need to arrange the rental, the pick up, and the return of all rental items. If you are using a ward house and using their tables, you need to arrange for someone to go in and set them up.

If the decorator isn't going to do it, you need to arrange for someone to set up the centerpieces. This is a small enough thing that someone in the wedding party could probably do it for you. But again, don't assume. Find a specific person and ask her to perform this specific task. This will better ensure its completion.

❑ Arrange for cleanup of centerpieces

Make sure this person knows what to do with the centerpieces after the reception.

Tip: Sometimes the centerpieces are given as a thank you to bridesmaids or people helping with the wedding.

chapter twenty

flowers

At the temple: The temple requests that corsages and boutonnieres be left at home and saved for the reception. The only exception to this is that the bride may bring her bouquet for outside the temple, and the groom may wear his boutonniere. All other flowers are considered reception attire and belong there. Even mothers' corsages. Remember to think, "Shouldn't I respect the temple regulations to help keep this a sacred experience?"

☒ Decide on <u>fresh</u> or silk

Fresh flowers are beautiful but much more expensive, up to two or three times the cost of silk flowers. Fresh are essentially disposable, while silk can be kept for years to come. All the flowers don't have to be the same. The bride's bouquet could be fresh and everything else silk. Or the bouquet and the groom's boutonniere could be fresh and the rest silk, or add the moms' corsages to the fresh side. You could even mix fresh and silk around the room; most people won't notice. It's totally open for discussion. It's all based on your personal preferences. If you do use fresh flowers, it will save you money to choose flowers that are in season.

❑ Decide who will receive
  boutonnieres and corsages

You'll need to decide who will wear them so you can get a definite count. If you're afraid you're wrong, you could order an extra of each just in case.

Normally you would order a bride's bouquet and a groom's boutonniere, and then move out in stages from there. It's a good idea to also set a line and be consistent with who gets a corsage or boutonniere. For instance, don't get the bride's mom one, but not the groom's mom. One line could be groom's mom and dad, bride's mom and dad. Another line could be anyone else in the line or add grandparents. And last moving out to immediate siblings or the entire wedding party. A good guideline of where you should draw the line will be budget. If you have ample budget and want to go the extra mile, some brides have their bridesmaids, sisters, or mothers each hold a small bouquet or even a single flower, instead of having corsages. This is definitely an extravagance and won't be expected, but it can be fun.

❑ Decide on one bridal bouquet or two
(so one may be thrown and one kept)

Some brides like to keep their bouquets. That's great—just have a second one made so that you can throw it to all the single ladies at the reception.

❑ Arrange for florist/flowers

You'll need to decide who's going to do the flowers—whether it's a florist, you, or a family member.

Note! A florist can be used even if you are doing silk flowers.

Then you'll need to hire the florist or purchase the flowers to be arranged. Before you decide on someone, ask to see samples or at least photos of their personal work. If you are hiring a florist, then the next two checkboxes will be easily done; just tell her what you need and when. (Don't forget to add in the centerpieces if you are going with flowers for them.)

Note! Arrange for the flowers to be picked up or delivered

Decide what flowers you would like to use. Take a swatch of fabric in your wedding color to help you keep it in mind. What do you want the bouquet and such made out of? Do you have a favorite flower? Are you open to suggestions from the florist? Ask a friend of yours who loves flowers what some of her favorites are. Go walk through a flower shop or even the silk flower aisle at Walmart. Look at options and have fun. Some flowers send a different message than others. Sunflowers, for example, are much friendlier and informal while roses are more elegant and classic. When choosing the flowers, be conscious of their scents. Some flowers' scents are stronger than others. You don't want to overwhelm your guests.

Tip: Mix foliage and even fruit into the arrangements to add variety. You can also use petals instead of full flowers for decorating to cut back on cost.

Don't forget to order any of the flowers that may be associated with your headpiece, centerpieces, or cake.

❑ Arrange corsages and boutonnieres

If a florist is being used, this task is pretty easy. If not, you'll want to make sure that the corsages and boutonnieres get done.

❑ 🛇 Arrange for bridal bouquet

Again, if a florist is being used, easy-peasy. If not, just make sure the bouquet gets made.

❑ Arrange for flowers to be removed

Make sure everyone knows if they can keep their personal flowers and that someone knows what to do with the extra flowers. (For example: return them all to your home, send them home with guests, donate them to a nursing home.)

chapter twenty-one

music

☐ **Determine reception music**

Decide if you want the reception music to be live entertainment or recorded music played.

☐ **Arrange for someone to maintain music or for DJ, if recorded**

Ask someone specific to maintain the music. That could be either a DJ-type setup or as simple as streaming a playlist from your MP3 player through the sound system at the venue. But either way, someone should be in charge of it so that should a problem arise, it can be solved quickly.

☐ **Arrange for entertainment, if live**

If you decide you want live music, you'll need to choose and schedule a band. The "band" could be one piano player, all the way to a full live band or orchestra. You can use friends or, if you're near a college or university, there's likely to be many amateur groups willing to perform for cheap, if not free. Think about your guests again and what would make them feel comfortable. Think about background music and dancing music. What are your needs?

Once you decide what you want, you'll need to make sure the reception venue can accommodate them before booking them. Then ask the band questions. Make sure you know what will be included in the price. Is it hourly or by the gig? Will there be continuous music or do they require breaks? See what they are like when they perform. Watch a tape or make a date of it and go see them at another gig. Once you've made your choice, book the band.

Then, after booking them, you'll need to make sure they have everything they need made available to them, such as a piano or microphones.

❏ Determine playlist

You'll need to decide what music you want played. It usually takes a while to compile and generally narrow down the music you want played, so begin this process early. This way you can begin creating a playlist if using recorded music, and you can alert the band if you are using live music. Remember, if using a live band, you generally don't dictate every single song they will play. You'll want to make sure the band is amenable to the playlist or even if they can play your desired songs at all. Be open to their suggestions; they may have some. If you have some you definitely don't want played, kindly ask that those songs be removed from their repertoire.

Decide which songs you want played for your first and last dances. Do you want a certain style during dinner and then something else for the dancing? Ask the band and other friends and family members for suggestions from their playlist. If you are using recorded music and you don't want to arrange the playlist yourself, you can buy romantic compilation CDs for just this occasion. Remember to bring your cords for charging if you are using an MP3 player.

Think about what your guests are comfortable with and what is appropriate if your venue is the church. Your parents are likely not your same age and probably don't like the same exact music you like. Be sensitive to that, as your guests will be a varied group. One idea may be to play some older, more conservative music toward the beginning and then let the rock-and-roll loose later in the night. The younger guests are going to be the ones who stick it out to the end anyway. Overall, remember that when you're talking volume, many guests will want to keep visiting throughout the entire night.

❑ Arrange for sound system at venue

You will need a sound system not only for your music but also so you can have a microphone available. You will want a microphone for any announcements, including: introduction of the couple, cutting the cake, throwing the bouquet, throwing the garter, the couple's departure, dancing, or even an emergency. You'll be glad you don't have to shout over the guests to make any announcements.

If you are using a church, they have a built-in sound system so you're set. But you will want to test it and make sure you have access to it. If you're having the reception at a reception center, they'll likely have arrangements for this as well. However, if you are having your reception somewhere unique or anywhere outside, you'll have to think of a way to get a sound system there and make sure it's loud enough to hear the music but not so loud that your guests can't visit or that the neighbors complain.

❑ Test sound at reception venue

If you're music is live, the band will probably test their sound the night of, but it's still a good idea to have an idea of what the sound is like at your venue. You'll want to do this no matter what sort of venue you are using. Contact the person connected to the venue to try out your music early. Buildings and especially non-buildings do strange things to sound, like swallow it up or echo it back at you. That's the kind of thing you'll want to know before you try to stuff in three hundred people.

❑ Arrange for an MC

This could be a member of the band, the DJ, the best man, or anyone else. You'll want to have someone that will be assigned to make any necessary announcements. Make sure the MC knows what they are going to announce and when that is expected. Make a timetable. Don't wait for a break in the line or a lull in the conversation. Have a plan and stick to it.

If you are having dancing you will want to let your MC know about any special dances as well (for example: the bridal couple's first dance, father/daughter dance, mother/son dance, and so on).

chapter twenty-two

guest registry

❑ Determine guest book

Decide if you want your guests to sign some sort of guest registry and, if so, how you want it to look. It is nice to have a list later of who came to the reception.

You can simply purchase a "wedding guests" book from a store, or you can get creative and invent a way for the guests to sign their name. There are many options, from different kinds of books, to a large picture frame, to names in a bottle. You can create a scrapbook for them sign or have small papers to write a message to the bridal couple on.

Here's the key: make sure there's enough space for all the guests to sign (remember some will write messages as well). If you're having an intimate party with twenty people, the picture frame might be great. There is, however, not a frame really conducive to three hundred signatures.

❑ Arrange for guest book

This check box is for you to assign the responsibility of creating the guest book to someone. This is something that you could easily do yourself well before the wedding day, or you could simply purchase one.

❑ Arrange for guest book display

Think about how you want the guest book to be made available to your guests. It's a good idea to put it near the entrance so they can sign it right as they walk in or even while they wait in line to see the couple. If you want all your guests to sign, then you'll want the book displayed prominently.

The guest book is generally set on a table, so you need to decide if you want other things on the table. Attract attention to it so it will not go unnoticed. You could have the same centerpieces as the other tables, but most people decorate it specially. It is common to have a picture of the bride, at least, but I prefer one of the couple together. This table is a place to have a little more fun with the decorations. You'll definitely need a pen (not a bad idea to have a few, just in case one runs out of ink). Some families will place a video of the bride and groom through the years near the book.

❑ Arrange for someone to attend/ maintain guest book

It is a good idea to have someone maintain the guest book. By maintain, I mean simply turn the pages and make sure the pen gets changed out when it runs out of ink. This is a good job for that friend that is nine months pregnant and desperately wants to help. She can sit down the whole reception. It can also be done by someone who just checks in on the book regularly but wanders the reception the rest of the time. But make sure this person understands that she must check in on the book regularly. I have seen people pass up the book without signing because the page was full. Really, like it never occurred to them to turn the page.

❑ Arrange for the guest book to be removed

Just figure out where the guest book is going and who is making sure it gets there. My bet is it's going to end up with the couple . . . just a guess.

Idea: It can be great to add some things to your guest book after the event, such as

- physical things about you (how old you are, what you weigh, how tall you are, what color you hair is)
- some of your favorites
- some of your feelings from your wedding day
- an experience from your day that was funny or went wrong
- plans for your future together

These can all be fun things to look back on later, and you'll be glad you wrote them down.

chapter twenty-three

gifts

❑ Determine how gifts will be accepted and placed

In some areas it is very common to display the gifts given to the bridal couple. In other places that is considered taboo. You should do what suits you and suits the area you live in. If you don't want the gifts displayed, you will still need to arrange for them to be taken and placed somewhere.

If you decide to have the gifts displayed, decide if you want a table set out for the guests to set the gifts on or if you want someone to take them from the guests and then place them on the table. Make sure there is plenty of room for many gifts. Do you want the gifts opened? Or displayed as they come?

✍ **Note!** If you have someone open your gifts for you, make sure they keep a detailed list of which gift came from whom so you can still write thank you cards later.

It is inappropriate to put out a bowl and sign requesting money. It is, however, very appropriate to have a place to put cards. If you decide you want to have little tiny boys accept gifts, just make sure they will actually bring them back to the table and not open them. Also, have a couple of adults help them, because several gifts will be too heavy or fragile to hand to a small child.

❑ Arrange for gift area at reception

Decide where the gifts will be placed and arrange for it to be set up. This could be a long table with just a tablecloth set on it. It could be a corner at the reception with several small tables or even a gazebo. Just make sure someone is assigned to set it up. The decorator generally takes care of this.

It is a good idea to have a place for people to put cards as well. Many people bring cards with checks and gift cards in lieu of a large, boxy gift. It will be easier to keep track of the cards in a set place than along the gift table, in the groom's pocket, or kicking around the dance floor. This place for cards can easily be a small basket or box possibly decorated with a small sign that states simply, "CARDS."

❑ Arrange for someone to accept gifts/maintain gift table

Ask people to accept gifts and maintain the gift table. By maintain, I mean accept gifts, make sure no one bothers them, and watch carefully any money envelopes that are dropped off. This person would also manage any helpers you have accepting gifts for you. My suggestion is to have the person at the gift table securely tape the card to every gift. Every gift. Even if it's already taped. And I wouldn't use scotch tape, I'd use packing tape. This is to keep the cards with the gifts, which will help when you're writing thank you notes.

❑ Arrange for someone to transport gifts

These people will need to carefully pack up the gifts at the end of the night and take them to a safe place for you until after you get back from your honeymoon. The groom's attendants are a fine choice for this job. If you don't have attendants, you can ask brothers and fathers or even your elder's quorum. They could take them to either your house or their house, just somewhere the gifts will be left alone. There will be a lot of gifts, so you'll need someone with a van or a covered truck bed. And you'll need to remind them to take care with the gifts and also try to make sure the cards stay on.

Sometime after your honeymoon, you'll want to open your

gifts. You'd think this a simple thing, and it should be. It isn't though. Many people decide to make a hoopla out of the gift opening as well. Some couples invite the whole family to watch the opening of the gifts, while other couples invite both sets of parents to watch the opening of presents. If both of your families are the kind who really want to be a part of this, then go right ahead. My personal opinion is:

! Soapbox Warning

All right. Don't make people come watch you open your gifts. That is ridiculous. If they want to—they really want to—then okay, try to find some middle ground, but don't make them. Like your baby sister wants to sit around for hours—and it will be hours—to watch you open a million gifts. Your wedding gifts are wonderful and super fun for you and maybe your mom, but they are overall boring to most others. People will care about some of the things you get. But everything? No. My best idea is just write down what people give you so that when Mom asks, "What did Aunt Laurel give you?" you can politely and gratefully respond, "Oh, Mom! She gave me the loveliest vacuum. It's exactly what I always wanted. She's so awesome."

See how that's better? Now you and your groom can take your time opening your gifts. This will also give you a chance to openly say what you really think about each gift instead of filtering your responses. It really is a fun time for you and your groom to take time thinking about each gift and where you'll put it and how very thoughtful it was of the giver.

chapter twenty-four

bridal shower

This only has a brief mention on the wedding checklist because it is not the responsibility of anyone that is planning the wedding to plan the bridal shower (neither of the mothers and definitely not the bride herself). However, it has a chapter because there are several things to remember when deciding what to do. Bridal showers are a great way for members of each family to meet one another.

First (For the Bride)

Don't blindly say "yes" to everyone who offers to give you a shower. Thank them for the offer, and don't instantly accept. You really shouldn't have more than one shower. However, if you do have more than one, absolutely don't overlap the guest lists. Your ward may decide to throw you a shower, or your friends, or your family. But don't have your friends invited to your ward shower and your friend shower. It is greedy and presumptuous to ask people to attend two showers. You may think, "Hey, I'm giving them options," but that isn't how it is received by your guests. Also, it is difficult for the hostess to plan if the guests are choosing between two showers to attend. They may all choose to go to one and no one goes to the other—not nice to the hostess. Better to let just one person do a shower and invite everyone.

❑ Make a list of attendees with their addresses

Your job as the bride is to provide the hostess with a guest list and addresses, if necessary, and to be grateful to her for all her efforts, time, and money donated to honoring you. Be careful to give the hostess a very real number of guests. Be considerate of her plans and the time and money she's spending. Think about all your friends and family when telling her how many people you have to invite, so she can plan accordingly. Don't tell her a number and then continue to contact her with more and more people. That can make it difficult to plan.

You won't always have to provide a guest list, though. If a member of the ward gives you a shower, they'll already know the members of the ward and so will need nothing from you but to show up. If your sister is giving you the shower, she'll know all of your family and will only need from you the groom's number to get his family's info, or potentially she'll need a friend guest list from you. See? Little stress for you.

One thing you can do is just accept the first person that offers and then tell everyone else you're already having a shower and add them to your shower guest list. That makes it so you don't have to choose. But be careful, the first person that offers may not be the best person for the job. The person throwing the shower should be close to you, the bride, and know you.

A few tips: Be on time to your shower; send thank you cards as soon as possible; include a special thank you to your hostess, even if she doesn't give you a gift. (The shower took time and money and more than a little love for you.)

One last thing: your groom is not invited to your shower. Traditionally you would wear all the bows from your gifts and at the end of your shower your groom would come pick you up, and he'd give you a kiss for every bow.

Second (To the Hostess of the Shower)

Think about what kind of shower you want to do. Guests, theme, invitations, time and place, gifts, games, and food.

Guests

Who do you want at the shower? Is it a family shower? Friends? Ward? How many people are you inviting? If it's a combined shower, get guest suggestions from the bride and from both the mother of the bride and the mother of the groom. Make sure you get a full list and their addresses. That way you can move ahead with the invitations and other preparations.

Tip: It's a fun idea to have a guest book to pass around for all the guests to sign, or to at least have someone write down everyone who came. It's fun to look back years later and remember who came to your shower.

Theme

Your shower does not need a theme, but you may choose one. The theme is usually tied to the kind of gifts you are hoping for, such as "Around the clock," where each guest is given a time of day and the gift is supposed to match that time. Be careful—this can get naughty; and the bad side is that if someone doesn't come, you miss a time.

Other themes could be seasons, holidays, or simply personal, bed and bath, kitchen, holiday or my personal favorite "stock the pantry." Whatever the theme, make sure that if it's tied to the gifts, that is made clear in the invitation. Don't assume every guest is going to call you for clarification.

! Soapbox Warning

I personally do not like bridal showers being tied to things like Pampered Chef® and Tupperware®. I think the point of the shower is for the bride to sit with her girlfriends and be giddy and talk about being married. I don't want to be interrupted in my celebrating with my friend or sister or daughter because I have to listen to some sales pitch. It's like a fly in the soup. "Sure, you can come have fun and celebrate. You just have to be harassed into buying a gift from a supplier that you would not have chosen in a place where everyone knows how much you paid for it." That could be intimidating.

Invitations

This is where you get to use your scrapbooking skills. Make them cute and frilly if you want, but make them clear to the guests and not too busy. Make your theme or gift suggestions clear. You may want to add the information that a meal will be served if it is the case. Don't forget to invite the bride.

Time and place

Choose a time that will be most convenient for all involved, but mostly for you and the bride. Think about what food you want to serve when you decide the time of day. Noon implies food will be served, as does 5:00 p.m. You may want to have an open house or a standard come and stay the whole time. If you put an end time on the invitation, people will assume it's an open house and will come anytime within the time frame. So if you want them to come and stay the duration of the shower, then just put a start time on the invitation.

Choose a place that can hold as many people as you hope for. Think about your decorations and your food being served when deciding a location. Often the shower is held either at the hostess's house or at a nearby church. But it can be held many places, such as a park, restaurant, or clubhouse.

Gifts

Many people choose their theme based on some gift idea. So these tend to go hand-in-hand. My suggestion for opening gifts would be to do it throughout the length of the shower. That way, each gift will get the attention and thanks it's due instead of a quick thanks and on to the next one. Whichever way you decide to open gifts, make sure it is someone's specific job to write down all the gifts and the givers for the bride. It is surprisingly difficult to remember even just a few gifts, and she will need that list later when writing her thank you notes.

Games

Think about your bride when you decide games. Will she be a good sport if the games embarrass her? Are you sure? Even if it's in front of her new in-laws? Are the games the kind that the guests will be willing to play, or will they be a hassle? You don't need games. You can just visit and open presents. However, if you're a game-playing family, go for it. This is one of those times that people tend to be more willing to play.

Food

This can be as big or small as you like—little snacks and treats or a full meal. Just decide what you'd like, how you're going to accomplish it, and make it happen. Plan enough for all the guests to show up; that way you won't run out just because you weren't expecting everyone.

Last thing

Remember that the bridal shower is to honor the bride—not to embarrass her. Choose things that she would like and that would make her feel comfortable. It can be difficult to combine different aspects of your life, such as family and friends.

Note! Groom showers are becoming more and more popular. No, not a bachelor party—a groom's shower. Like a bridal shower, but for the groom. This is an opportunity for the groom to receive BBQ's, camping gear, air filters, oil, and other suitable manly gifts. While this is not common in many places, if you want to do it, I say . . . sure!

chapter twenty-five

honeymoon

❑ Arrange for a place for the wedding night

Groom: You're responsible for the entire honeymoon. You'll need a place to go for the wedding night.

Usually by the end of the wedding day, you are tired and not planning on heading straight out on a flight or long car drive or boat or whatever for your honeymoon. So you need a place to go for that night. I urge you not to try to stay with someone or drive too far. Choose a motel or hotel or castle that is close to the reception and sweet and elegant for you. If you have an early flight, look for one close to the airport so you don't have to rush. Choose a place where you can be as comfortable as possible. This is not a time to choose the cheapest, dingiest place you can stand. Be sure to check reservations carefully. Make sure you are booking exactly what you think you're booking.

Tip: You can often find better deals by booking far in advance.

❑ Determine honeymoon destination

Decide where you are going to go on your honeymoon. It doesn't need to be grand. The couple themselves usually pays for the honeymoon. Don't spend all your money on the honeymoon. You'll need some for your life after the wedding.

Some couples don't even go on honeymoons anymore. While I

don't think a honeymoon should be too costly, I do think you should have one. Definitely. Where you go is not as important as being alone together. But choose someplace where you'll be comfortable. It's not the time to save a buck by staying in a roach motel.

There are so many options. You can go camping, snorkeling, hiking, skiing, or to Disneyland. But don't overschedule yourselves. Leave time to laze around in your hotel room. Talk to one another about what you are hoping for: a long stay or an exotic location. You may have to choose one or the other based on budget.

The most important thing about the honeymoon is that it's a time when you can be alone together and bask in the exciting start of a new phase in your life. Give yourselves a few days of basking before you jump into the odds and ends of normal life.

❑ Book a hotel for the honeymoon

After you've made a destination decision, choose a hotel and book it. Choose a comfortable one; it's likely you'll spend quite a bit of time there.

❑ Arrange for travel

Make travel arrangements to your destination city and any sight-seeing. If you require a flight, put your wife's ticket in her maiden name, since she will have to show her driver's license, and it needs to match the name on the ticket.

Whether or not you have a car, it's a good idea to plan a little extra money for cab fares or public transportation in case it better suits you at a different time in the trip.

✐ **Note!** Keep a detailed record of all your reservations and confirmation numbers. This will help things go smoothly should you hit a snag.

❑ Determine budget for meals and activities

It's a good idea to determine a budget before you go so you don't overspend. It'll be good practice for the beginning of your life together. Don't forget to add in extra money for tips and souvenirs.

❑ Ensure both passports and
   visas are set, if necessary

Again, make sure the visa is in your bride's maiden name to keep things running smooth.

❑ Pack for honeymoon

Have at least an overnight bag packed for the wedding night, plus any other bags for the duration of the trip. Remember, bride, you'll have lots of your essentials packed already for the temple trip. Remember to take your camera!

Groom: If your honeymoon destination is a surprise for your sweetheart, make it very clear to her what sort of things to pack. Big difference between a week in Maui, a week at the Grand Canyon, or a week at a ski lodge.

Tip: Leave a copy of your itinerary (with phone numbers where you can be reached) with someone trusted, in case of an emergency.

chapter twenty-six

living together

Don't forget in all the excitement of planning a wedding that when this whole thing is over, you'll be married. You'll want to prepare for life after the wedding as well.

❏ Make OB/GYN appointment

The bride should get a premarital check-up. Especially if you have never been to the obstetrician. This will include a pap-smear, breast cancer exam, and discussion of intimacy and contraceptives.

You need to schedule this appointment well in advance because it often takes a while to get into the OB. Many women choose to go to their mom's doctor for the first time. Some general practitioners will do this exam for you as well. If either of those makes you uncomfortable, you could ask your sisters or friends. It's important that you feel comfortable with the choice.

❏ Go to OB/GYN

Go to the OB appointment previously made.

❏ Arrange for birth control

I know it may be a bit embarrassing to talk about this before you're married, but you and your groom need to discuss your options. If you've already discussed your options, then your OB can help implement one of them. If you haven't discussed your options, then your OB can make suggestions that you and your groom will need to discuss, decide on, and implement.

❏ Arrange for time off work

Each of you (both the bride and the groom) will need to arrange with your boss for time off work. You may want to take the day before your wedding as well as the honeymoon after, but that's up to you.

❏ Arrange for time off school

If you are in college, you may be missing a few classes. You'll need to alert your professors, if necessary, and get any assignments needed as well as turn anything in. Just open your schedule.

❏ Write thank you notes for gifts as soon as you receive them

You are going to have to write lots and lots and lots of thank you notes. Once you get past your wedding, it will be overwhelming. The best method is to write thank you notes by hand personally and address them specifically to the giver as soon as you can for any gifts you receive before your wedding. This will give you a head start on at least a few dozen of them. The longer you wait, the harder it is to get it done. You could take a few of them with you when you go to the doctor's office or to have your oil changed. Do a few here and a few there. Trust me, writing them in stages will make the task a lot less overwhelming.

After the wedding, create a method for writing your notes. I think it is helpful as you open presents to write on the card what the gift is. Then keep all the cards together. You can use the cards as a reference for your thank you notes. This will help you be specific with your thank yous. As you write each thank you note, simply remove the giver's card from your stack. Then you'll know it's done. When you don't have any more cards from gifts, hopefully you've written all the thank you notes.

Another method is to keep a list (or spreadsheet) of who gave you what gifts and whether or not a thank you note has been sent. You could use your original guest list. This will help you be sure to get a note out to everyone, and it will also be a nice keepsake to have later. I'm amazed by which gifts I remember came from whom and which gifts I have no recollection of at all. Also, it helps to answer those questions from Mom. "What did Uncle Henry give you? What about Dad's boss?" or "How'd you like our gift?"

The standards for thank you notes are:
• they must be handwritten
• they must be personal
• they must mention what gift was given
• they must be sent, even if a verbal thank you was given already
• a group thank you note is appropriate if it was a group gift from coworkers
• individual thank you notes must be sent to all family and friends, even if they donated to a group gift

You should also write thank you notes to all the people who participated in your wedding in some capacity (for example: sat at the book, worked in the kitchen, lent you their dress).

Note! Don't go to all the trouble of writing the thank you notes and never mail them. My advice would be to mail them as you write them. Don't wait for them all to be done to send them. Then if you forget to send some, only a few people get missed instead of everyone. Truly: better late than never.

Many think it's necessary to have thank you gifts for your attendants, parents, and other members of the wedding party. I didn't give this a checkbox because I don't think it's common enough to be expected, especially since we don't always use attendants. You do not have to get gifts for everyone. It used to be the traditional thing to get a gift for each of your attendants, but this is going out of practice. If you do choose to do it, you can do something small. It doesn't require a lot of money—just something simple to say thank you, such as, embossed stationary, a small book, or a framed photo of the two of you.

Some couples are starting to give gifts to their parents following the wedding, also as a thank you. Don't do this. It's totally not necessary. Anything they gave you, whether time or money, was a gift. If you want to say thank you, which is a very nice thing, then a simple note is really the best choice.

❑ Find a place to live

It's inevitable that you'll need a place. Just find one and secure it.

✍ **Caution:** If one of you moves into your future home prior to your marriage, never spend time alone there without a chaperone. You may think you're strong, but Satan is determined to ruin this for you. And he is cunning.

❑ Shop for new home furniture

Don't go nuts with this. You don't need to run out to IKEA and bet the farm. You would probably like at least a bed though. Just a thought.

❑ Arrange for utilities to be turned on

Some apartments include utilities. Just make sure all utilities are turned on and in your name. Then when you move in you'll have those pesky things like water, electricity, and phone.

❑ Move your stuff

You're going to need to actually move into your new place. Pack up your stuff, transport it, and drop it off at the new place. Remember not to go unchaperoned. Give yourself some time to do this. It takes longer than you'd think to go through a life's worth of collected math papers.

❑ Change address, if necessary

You'll want to change your address with the post office so you get your mail at your new home.

❑ Change name

Change name on driver's license, school ID, social security card, passport, credit cards, library card, insurance, voter registration, banks, ward records, car registration, leases, and so on (can be done later).

This is a step best saved for after the wedding. Really, it's like you've lost your wallet. You need to catch any company that knows your name.

❑ Arrange for health and car insurance

You'll need to make sure you're all set up with health insurance if you don't already have it. Also, add each other to your car insurance, or get your own if you're still on Mom and Dad's.

❑ Change cell phone plans

You don't necessarily have to change, but you may want to add one or the other of you to the other's cell phone plan, making calling your spouse easier.

❑ Open a joint bank account

You're your own couple now. Open a joint bank account. If for nothing else, you'll need it to cash all those wedding checks written out to Mr. and Mrs. (groom's name).

conclusion

We are told in the scriptures, "Men are that they might have joy" (2 Ne. 2:25). Joy is God's plan for us. What better way to bring joy into our lives, sisters, than by sealing ourselves to a truly wonderful man for eternity and starting a new family. This is our path.

I know this seems like a lot of stuff just to plan a party. It is. But as you make decisions, you'll be surprised how fast some things check off. And there's something satisfying about checking that box. Really. It's been scientifically proven.

You can do it. Remember that very little here is necessary. Most of it is bells and whistles, and we like bells and whistles sometimes; but the only thing that matters in the end is that you're married, and that is such a beautiful and spiritual thing. Across the nation, we as Latter-day Saints value marriage more then a wedding. Isn't that the way it's supposed to be? I love it!

Man (and woman!) was not meant to be alone. We need one another, so we join ourselves together to build families and to bring them back to our Eternal Father. He loves us, and we love Him. May we find time each day to remember Him, and all the details of the planning will remain in perspective. Thank you for giving me your time, and congratulations on the beginning of the most exciting, important, and necessary path you have ever embarked upon.

resources

As I have previously stated, there are many resources out there for you. Check your local directory and the Internet. Ask around and look at magazines. Here are a few resources that I find helpful.

Overall wedding ideas and planning:
- www.latterdaybride.com
- www.weddinglds.com

What to expect from an LDS wedding:
- http://lds.org/liahona/2004/10/planning-your-temple -wedding?lang=eng
- http://www.ldschurchtemples.com/mormon/weddings/

Temple Location Information:
- www.ldschurchtemples. You can even print out driving directions straight from this site

Helping family understand a temple wedding:
- http://lds.org/ensign/2005/02/questions-and-answers?lang=eng

appendix a
the checklist

Communications
- ☑ Decide for yourselves (the couple) what type of wedding you are hoping for
- ☑ Parents of bride and groom meet together with the bride and groom to determine the overall budget and how the expenses will be shared
- ☑ Decide who's in charge
- ☐ Double and maybe even triple check all reservations and arrangements

Budget
- ☑ Make a prioritized rough budget
- ☑ Set a clear & specific budget

Before Invitations
- ☑ Set a date
- ☑ Determine the wedding party
- ☑ Make a tentative "months to the wedding" schedule
- ☑ Make a tentative "day of" schedule
- ☑ Choose a temple
- ☑ Schedule the temple
- ☑ Take engagement photos

☑ Register with a store
☑ Arrange wedding luncheon location
☑ Choose a time for the luncheon
☑ Select a place for reception
☑ Reserve reception venue
☑ Select engagement photo
☐ Print engagement photos
☑ Decide reception time

Invitations

☑ Compile guest lists
☑ Plan accommodations for out-of-town guests
☑ Choose invitations
☑ Determine invitation wording and layout
☑ Determine if RSVPs are needed and order them
☑ Order wedding invitations
☑ Prepare a map for invitation, if applicable
☑ Purchase thank you cards
☐ Decide on and order "luncheon" invitations
☐ Address and mail "luncheon" invitations
☑ Find addresses for everyone on guest lists
☑ Address wedding invitations
☑ Mail invitations

Ceremony

☐ Get marriage license
☑ Choose & ask your ceremony witnesses
☑ Choose & ask your escort
☑ Schedule appointment with bishop and stake president for a living ordinance recommend
☑ Meet with bishop and stake president to obtain living ordinance recommend
☑ Make arrangements for and receive endowments, if needed
☑ Make arrangements for "day of" transportation
☐ Pack for temple trip
☑ Bring rings to temple

- ❏ Iron temple packet
- ☑ Finalize your "day of" schedule
- ❏ Make sure all immediate family members have a "day of" schedule

Ring Ceremony

- ☑ Determine if having a ring ceremony
- ☑ Determine how ring ceremony will be presented
- ☑ Choose a place for the ring ceremony
- ☑ Determine a time for the ring ceremony
- ☑ Determine who will conduct the ring ceremony

Wedding Luncheon

- ☑ Choose a time for the luncheon (if not previously done)
- ☑ Choose a luncheon venue (if not previously done)
- ❏ Prepare and send luncheon invitations (if not previously done)
- ☑ Determine who will prepare, serve and clean-up the food
- ☑ Choose a serving style and menu
- ☑ Determine which dishes will be used & how they will get there
- ☑ Purchase food (if not done by professional)
- ❏ Determine how decorations will be done
- ☑ Determine how entertainment will be handled

Photography

- ☑ Select a photographer
- ☑ Schedule photographer for wedding day
- ❏ Meet with photographer to discuss shots
- ☑ Schedule bridal shoot (if desired)
- ☑ Have bridal shoot (if applicable)
- ☑ Ask someone to assist photographer
- ☑ Decide how you'll share other candid shots

Videography

- ☑ Select a videographer

- ☑ Schedule a videographer
- ☑ Meet with videographer to discuss shots

Rings

- ☑ Purchase bride's engagement ring/wedding band set
- ☑ Purchase groom's ring
- ☑ Pick up rings from sizing/engraving

Wedding Dress

- ☑ Select wedding gown
- ☑ Purchase/rent/sew/acquire wedding gown
- ☑ Select and acquire headpiece
- ☑ Select and acquire accessories
- ☑ Select and acquire shoes
- ☑ Plan for the weather
- ☑ Acquire undergarments
- ☑ Have dress altered and temple ready
- ☑ Purchase garter
- ☑ Have your hair cut or dyed, if desired
- ☑ Practice doing hair with veil
- ☑ Have a final wedding dress fitting
- ☑ Have bride pampering time

Groom's Attire

- ☑ Choose groom's tuxedo
- ☑ Arrange for groom's tuxedo
- ☑ Arrange for groom's shoes
- ☐ Groom's haircut
- ☐ Pick up groom's tuxedo
- ☐ Groom's final fitting

Family & Attendants Attire

- ☑ Determine who is wearing tuxedos
- ☑ Arrange for family tuxedos
- ☐ Pick up family tuxedos

- [ ] Return all rented tuxes
- [x] Decide mothers' dresses
- [x] Arrange for mothers' dresses
- [x] Decide on wedding family/attendant attire
- [x] Decide family's & attendants' shoes
- [ ] EVERYONE try on their wedding attire

Reception

- [x] Determine type of reception
- [x] Decide on a color
- [x] Map out the reception layout
- [x] Determine reception program
- [ ] Print a written program, if desired
- [ ] Ask people to help at reception; assign specific jobs
- [x] Determine wedding receiving line
- [x] Ask members of line to join
- [x] Select room for bride and groom to change clothing
- [x] Make a plan for children at reception
- [ ] Arrange for bride/groom departure

Food

- [x] Choose and hire a caterer OR choose and arrange for food help
- [x] Select menu for reception
- [x] Determine how food will be prepared
- [x] Determine how food will be distributed
- [x] Decide what reception "paper or china" goods are needed
- [ ] Purchase reception plates, cups, utensils
- [x] Order or buy reception food
- [ ] Prepare reception food
- [ ] Arrange for cleanup of food and all food areas
- [ ] Determine what is to be done with leftovers
- [ ] Provide means to deal with leftovers

Cake

- [x] Decide if you will be serving the cake at the reception
- [x] Decide on a cake decorator

- ☑ Decide on a cake design
- ☑ Choose a cake topper
- ☑ Acquire a cake topper
- ☑ Order cake
- ☑ Arrange for cake to get to reception
- ☑ Purchase cake-cutting utensils
- ☑ Determine how cake will be displayed
- ☑ Determine when cake will be cut
- ☐ Determine how cake will be served and by whom
- ☑ Purchase cake serving goods
- ☐ Make arrangements for uneaten cake

Decorations

- ☐ Decide reception decorations and layout
- ☑ Check over lighting
- ☑ Determine flow of guests
- ☐ Arrange for reception decorations
- ☐ Arrange for reception venue to be decorated
- ☐ Arrange for decoration cleanup

Centerpieces

- ☑ Decide linens
- ☑ Decide centerpieces
- ☑ Create, buy, or borrow centerpieces
- ☐ Arrange for centerpieces/table setup
- ☐ Arrange for cleanup of centerpieces

Flowers

- ☑ Decide fresh or silk
- ☑ Decide who will receive boutonnieres and corsages
- ☑ Decide on one bouquet or two
- ☑ Arrange for florist/flowers
- ☑ Arrange corsages and boutonnieres
- ☑ Arrange for bridal bouquet
- ☐ Arrange for flowers to be removed

Music

- ☑ Determine reception music
- ☑ Arrange for someone to maintain music or for DJ, if recorded — Alyse
- ☑ Arrange for entertainment, if live
- ☑ Determine playlist
- ☐ Arrange for sound system at venue
- ☐ Test sound at reception venue
- ☑ Arrange for an MC

Guest Book

- ☑ Determine guest book
- ☐ Arrange for guest book
- ☐ Arrange for guest book display
- ☑ Arrange for someone to attend/maintain guest book
- ☑ Arrange for the the guest book to be removed

Gifts

- ☑ Determine how gifts will be accepted and placed → Aub & Mic watch
- ☑ Arrange for gift area at reception
- ☐ Arrange for someone to accept gifts/maintain gift table
- ☐ Arrange for someone to transport gifts

Bridal Shower

- ☑ Make a list of attendees with their addresses

Honeymoon

- ☑ Arrange for a place for the wedding night
- ☑ Determine honeymoon destination
- ☑ Book a hotel for honeymoon
- ☑ Arrange for travel
- ☐ Determine budget for meals and activities
- ☑ Ensure both passports and visas are set, if necessary
- ☐ Pack for honeymoon

Living Together

- ☑ Make OB/GYN appointment
- ☑ Go to OB/GYN
- ☑ Arrange for birth control
- ☑ Arrange for time off work
- ☑ Arrange for time off school
- ☐ Write thank you notes for gifts as soon as you receive them
- ☑ Find a place to live
- ☐ Shop for new home furniture
- ☑ Arrange for utilities to be turned on
- ☐ Move your stuff
- ☐ Change address, if necessary
- ☐ Change name
- ☐ Arrange for health and car insurance
- ☑ Change cell phone plans
- ☐ Open a joint bank account

appendix b
the schedule

Months to the Wedding

Here is a general idea of when to schedule everything. My checklist is not necessarily in order of when it should be done. Obviously all the "Before Invitations" section should be done before invitations. This schedule will help you get things done as quickly as possible. I'll be using two months as a premise as I think that's about the quickest you can still get the whole hoopla taken care of within etiquette rules. If you have more time, great! It's always easier to add time than to take it away.

Keep in mind, if you are trying to plan a wedding in two months, it's about the only thing you'll be doing. This is really fast and requires you to be decisive and act quickly. It also usually means recruiting quite a bit of help; but one thing I know is that across the nation, we as Mormons are quick to help.

First of all, give everyone as much time as possible for whatever they have to accomplish. Make a decision as quickly as possible and alert the involved parties as soon as a decision has been made.

Second, the dates in this sample schedule are completion dates. You do not start the checkbox on that day, you need to have it *completed* by then, at the latest. If you have more time than two months, spread it out, but you still need a schedule based on and around the invitations.

157

Two Months Before (Nine Weeks)
- ☑ Have parent/budget meeting
- ☑ Set a date
- ☑ Schedule temple
- ☑ Take engagement photos
- ☑ Choose a time
- ☑ Book reception venue
- ☑ Begin guest lists

Eight Weeks Before
- ☑ Schedule all your professional help (photographer, caterer, decorator, florist, cake decorator, band) or recruit non-professional help
- ☑ Start looking for a place to live
- ☑ Have all guest lists compiled
- ☑ Order invitations
- ☐ Order engagement photos

Seven Weeks Before
- ☑ If not using professional help, begin the work toward these areas: caterer, decorator, florist, cake decorator, band (that is, choose menu, begin gathering decorations, purchasing silk flowers to create corsages and so on)
- ☑ Prepare all invitation inserts
- ☑ Decide luncheon style and schedule venue
- ☑ Register with a store, if desired
- ☑ Begin to make decisions for the attire for the bride, groom and family

Six Weeks Before
- ☑ Meet with professional help to determine specifics or continue work if using non-professional help (photographer, caterer, decorator, florist, cake decorator, band)
- ☑ Receive the invitations and begin addressing them
- ☑ Choose luncheon food, decorations, setup, and program
- ☑ Schedule living ordinance and current temple recommend interviews

Five Weeks Before

☑ Mail invitations
☑ Book any rentals (including decorations, linens, transportation)
☑ Finalize all attire decisions and begin acquiring them
☑ Begin preparations for luncheon (shopping, decoration rentals or creation, program planning)

Four Weeks Before

☑ Confirm all professional help (photographer, caterer, decorator, florist, cake decorator, band)
☑ Between two and four weeks you do the smaller finishing details (confirm everyone that is non-professional help: family, friends, wedding line, and so on)
☑ Have all doctors visits done
☑ Book honeymoon

Three Weeks Before

☑ Between two and four weeks, do the smaller finishing details (confirm everyone that is non-professional help: family, friends, wedding line, and so on)
☑ Buy all rings and send them to be sized or engraved
☑ Arrange any out-of-town accommodations
❑ Obtain marriage license

Two Weeks Before

☑ Between two and four weeks, do the smaller finishing details (confirm everyone that is non-professional help: family, friends, wedding line, and so on)
☑ Confirm your time off work or school
☑ Write thank you notes as gifts come in

One Week Before

❑ Obtain both living ordinance recommends
☑ Make sure temple recommend is current
☑ Receive endowments, if not done previously
☑ Confirm tuxes
❑ Prepare temple clothes

☐ Confirm wedding night and honeymoon arrangements
☐ Pack
☐ Confirm all transportation arrangements for wedding day
☑ Confirm all services (professional and non-professional) and
  reservations
☐ Disperse copies of "day of" schedule

Wedding Eve

To-Do List:
☐ Pack for temple
☐ Pack for honeymoon
☐ Double check travel arrangements

The night before your wedding is a good time for each of you to spend some time with just your family. Your moms will really appreciate one last night dedicated to them.

Personally I didn't want to go the whole day without seeing my fiancé, so we spent time in the day together and then had an informal dinner that night shared with both families. (Just the family members living at home.) We then said our good-byes and left to be alone with our own families.

It is a good idea during the time leading up to your wedding, but especially the night before your wedding, to say your good-bye to your fiancé in chaperoned company. I know this may sound like a bit much, but trust me, especially the night before your wedding it can be hard. You don't want to get that close to a temple wedding and mess up. Better safe than sorry. Just say a polite good-bye with a chaste kiss in front of your mom and dad, and you'll be very safe.

Go to bed early. You are about to have a very big day. Get enough rest and relaxation. I know it can be hard to sleep because of anxiety or nerves or excitement. But go to sleep early. You don't want to fall asleep at the altar do you? Or miss your own wedding night because you're too exhausted? Believe me, you'll be glad you had a good night's sleep the night before.

Wedding Day

This is just a sample schedule; yours will depend entirely on the actual times of things on your wedding day. Let us pretend for this schedule that your wedding is at 10 a.m. and your reception is from 6 to 9 p.m. This is just an example.

A.M.

6:30 Get up/get ready (give yourself plenty of time to get ready and eat breakfast)

8:00 Pack up car (don't forget your emergency kit)

8:20 Leave for temple (leave yourself time for delays)

9:00 Check in at temple (bride, groom, both escorts, both witnesses)

9:30 Guests check in at temple (be specific as to which temple and give the address)

10:00 Ceremony

11:00 Pictures at temple (be specific as to who should stick around for this)

P.M.

12:30 Luncheon (be specific as to where, with the address)

2:00 Separate for rest and last-minute preps (bride and groom need to arrange a place to rest)

4:30 Meet at reception venue (be specific as to who should arrive at this time for reception pictures)

5:00 Reception pictures

6:00 Reception

7:30 Cut cake/throw bouquet and garter

8:00 Dancing

9:00 Reception over/change to leave

9:15 Bridal couple leaves/reception cleanup

✍ **One last note to the bride and her mother!**

It is in your best interest to plan so that you can spend the wedding day concentrating on the joy and excitement of the day. Try to allow yourself the time to enjoy this instead of planning to do a bunch of work yourselves on this day. Mom's official job should be escorting her daughter around and showing her off.

appendix c
sample budgets

For the Bride

Set your priorities. Where are you willing to spend more money? Where are you going to cut back? If you run short on money, what can you do without? There is no set amount that a wedding is supposed to cost. It all depends on what you can afford and what you're willing to pay. Remember: track every penny you spend. If you overspend in one place, you need to cut back somewhere else. This example is divided a traditional way, so make sure it is clear on your budget sheet who is paying for what.

Total Available Funds: _____

Wedding Coordinator:_____

Invitations (including thank you notes, any other inserts, and postage): _____

Photography (including all shoots and reprints): _____

Videography: _____

Reception Venue/Decorator/Decorations (including rentals):_____

Food (including catering and dishes):_____

Wedding Cake (including cutting and serving items): _____

Flowers (all flowers the bride is paying for, whether worn or used as decor in the room, with the food, or on the cake):_____

Music: _____

Accommodations: _____

Wedding Dress (including veil, accessories, shoes, and
possible gown preservation): _____

Family Dress:_____

Groom's Ring: _____

Transportation (whether a rented vehicle or gas to a
remote location):_____

Miscellaneous (including emergency funds): _____

These are your general categories. Take everything you want to
do, slot it into a category, or add a new category and take it from
"miscellaneous." But you need a starting point and a going-off-the-
cliff point.

Have a place for amount budgeted, amount paid, and outstand-
ing balance. Keep track of all expenses and receipts in case anything
goes wrong. Be very clear with anyone else spending your wedding
budget as to how much is allotted for that specific thing.

For the Groom

Total available funds: _____

Bride's ring: _____

Groom's attire (including shoes, cleaning fee): _____

Tuxedos (all other bridal party tuxedos): _____

Luncheon: Food(including dishes): _____

Decor(including linens): _____

Entertainment: _____

Marriage license (including blood tests if your
state requires them): _____

Bride's bouquet: _____

Corsages and boutonnieres (or whatever you have passed out to
the bridal party, such as bouquets or single flowers):_____

Honeymoon (including transportation and
wedding night):_____

Miscellaneous (including emergency funds): _____

appendix d

bride's emergency kit

You don't need to take all of this, but if you do, you'll probably have what you need.

For the Temple
- [ ] temple recommend (bride and groom)
- [ ] living ordinance recommend
- [ ] marriage license
- [ ] wedding dress
- [ ] wedding dress underclothes (slip, corset, stockings)
- [ ] wedding veil
- [ ] temple shoes
- [ ] packet (bride and groom)
- [ ] wedding rings
- [ ] groom's tux or suit (as he'll have to change for pictures)
- [ ] white handkerchief
- [ ] extra copies of directions
- [ ] phone numbers for all service help
- [ ] cell phones
- [ ] bridal bouquet (if you want it in pictures)

Toiletries
- [ ] makeup (including lipstick and powder)
- [ ] makeup remover
- [ ] fingernail care (polish, remover, clippers, file, glue)

- ❏ hair care (brush, comb, curling iron, gel, bobby pins, barrettes, hairspray)
- ❏ breath control (toothbrush, toothpaste, mouthwash, breath mints)
- ❏ tissues
- ❏ wet wipes
- ❏ lotion
- ❏ deodorant
- ❏ sunblock
- ❏ hand sanitizer
- ❏ Q-tips/cotton balls

Medicine
- ❏ pain pills (like aspirin or Tylenol)
- ❏ Band-Aids and triple antibiotic ointment
- ❏ antacid
- ❏ antihistamine
- ❏ any prescriptions (including inhaler)
- ❏ tampons/pads
- ❏ bottled water
- ❏ small snack (like a granola bar)

Fix-Its
- ❏ sewing kit (including: needle, thread, buttons, safety pins, scissors)
- ❏ lint roller
- ❏ hat pins (for corsages or boutonnieres)
- ❏ masking tape (you'd be surprised)
- ❏ tide pen
- ❏ extra pantyhose
- ❏ small umbrella

Oh, and don't forget everything I forgot.

appendix e

vendor contact list

It is a good idea to keep a current master list of all your vendors or helpers so you can easily reach someone if there is a problem. Add anyone you may need to contact throughout the process. I'd probably alphabetize it by title for easy reading. Here are a couple of examples:

❑ **Bishop**

Name _____

Address_____

Phone _____

Secondary phone _____

Email _____

❑ **Wedding Planner**

Name _____

Address _____

Phone _____

Secondary phone _____

Email _____

And so forth for each person. List your parents, your ecclesiastical leaders, all vendors, your maid of honor, his best man. Well . . . you get the idea.

notes

notes

notes

notes

notes

notes

notes

notes

notes

about the author

Ann Louise Peterson is passionate about weddings. Some may consider her love of wedding planning an obsession, but anyone who knows Ann knows she just enjoys making people happy. She lives in the Salt Lake area with her husband and five children.